Contents

Dr Ian Sutherland died 30 September 2002.

Ian Sutherland had been involved in researching and writing on substance misuse for most of his professsional life as a psychologist. Immediately prior to his sudden death Ian had submitted a publishing proposal and an almost complete manuscript to Russell House Publishing for approval. His original intention was that the book was for parents. However, following conversations with RHP it was agreed that the book should be targeted at a much wider audience, as it was felt that there are many other groups who would benefit from it and find it both useful and interesting.

Sadly Ian died suddenly before the book was completed. It is for this reason that references to quoted material have not been noted and most of those noted are of American origin. However, Ian's impressive publication list is included at the end of this book. As this book was based on several of his publications it should be possible to trace any missing references by way of this list. All the views expressed in this book are, as far as we are aware the author's own views.

Ann Wheal was enthusiastic about the proposal and had agreed to act as commissioning editor. She had been in contact with Ian and it is for this reason that she agreed to continue with the project to help prepare it for publication.

Preface

This is not a textbook. It has been written specifically to give an insight into adolescent substance abuse and to suggest how to try and prevent problems with drugs or alcohol from developing. It is far better to prevent a person from becoming an addict or an alcoholic than to wait until they have half destroyed their lives and the lives of those around them.

The book is designed to help anyone working or living with young people (such as parents, carers, social workers or youth workers) spot the warning signs of substance abuse and offer guidance on how to do something about it before it is too late.

It aims to provide information that is objective and un-biased. As such it does not have a political or hidden agenda and straightforwardly promotes an understanding of what is going on in our society in relation to substance abuse. There is an awful lot of hype and bias thrown at us on a daily basis about drugs and alcohol: much of it is wrong. This book sets out to cut through all that, and, to use a popular phrase, explode many of the myths surrounding substance abuse. In doing so it will, hopefully, offer some reassurance to those involved with young people.

About This Book

We read endless statistics about how many drugs our children are using and how much alcohol they are drinking. This book shows ways in which children and young adolescents can control the urge to use alcohol and drugs excessively.

The book is designed to help people to recognise that they may either have an existing problem or are prone towards developing a problem. In particular, it allows others to do the same on behalf of young people. This is achieved through a 'risk factor' or 'odds ratio' approach which lets a person be aware that they may be, say, five times as likely to develop a drink problem as a friend even if they drink exactly the same amount of alcohol or use the same types and quantities of drugs.

Above all, this book is intended to be pragmatic. It is relatively short and is written in eight chapters. It is the only work we are aware of that allows a reader to assess their susceptibility and the susceptibility of others, to addiction, tell them why they are at risk and then tell them how to do something about it before it is too late.

Chapter 1: outlines the book. It introduces the angles of the book, presents the beliefs of the author, and indicates the style in which the book will be written. In addition, it also defines words which will be used throughout the book.

Chapter 2: describes the use of drugs and alcohol throughout time and provides a capsule history of drug use since 5,000 BC to the present day and the 'War on Drugs'.

Chapter 3: looks at individual drugs and types of drugs (e.g. Ecstasy and heroin) and discusses how they work and some of the physical and psychological effects they have. These details have been included because it is felt that we cannot reasonably look at the level to which we are at risk without being informed about the things we are at risk from.

Chapter 4: There are many theories as to why people abuse drugs and alcohol; in fact there are far too many. This chapter discusses some of the main theories and presents an overall picture of current thinking. In common with the rest of the book, this chapter is not presented from an academic standpoint.

Chapter 5: We are bombarded with facts and figures about alcohol and drugs, many of them wildly inaccurate. Here we present figures on who is using what as found by both the author's work and by the work of others. The figures are presented in a simple and understandable way and draw a world-wide picture. Individual drug use amongst certain sections of society is discussed: for instance the extent of Ecstasy use compared with alcohol in teenage boys.

Chapter 6: discusses in detail the risk factors mentioned in the introduction. Each of the risk factors is discussed and its importance given an odds ratio. For instance, if a person has a genetic father who is an alcoholic it places them at twice the risk of becoming an alcoholic themselves compared with a similar person without an alcoholic father.

Chapter 7: shows how a person can assess their own, or their child's, risk of eventually developing an alcohol or other substance related problem. This is done by way of a questionnaire. At the end of the chapter the reader will be able to say that, for instance, they are at four times greater risk from alcoholism than the average person. Most importantly they will also be able to give the reason for this. For example, they may be able to say they are at risk because of low levels of self-esteem caused by low academic achievement coupled with living in an alcohol-abusing environment.

Chapter 8: This final chapter tells the reader the danger signs to watch out for and tells them what to do about it, taking into account the findings in the previous chapter. The book concludes with an overall summary.

Chapter 1

Introduction

The possibility of addiction is the price human beings pay for having developed the ability to respond to pleasure.

Throughout the world, but particularly the Western world, the number of people becoming reliant on chemical substances is increasing. This by itself should come as no great surprise: ever since humans have had the ability to understand that drugs exist, they have been using artificial ways to alter their state of consciousness.

There are many purposes behind this book:

- It is designed, primarily, to present anyone who is concerned about substance abuse with a useful overview of the whole area. In order to do this we will present a reasonably technical overview of substance abuse, but we will avoid going into too much depth wherever possible. There seem to be few books that sit happily between simplistic guides and the heavy-weight tomes designed for only a handful of scientists to read. By the end of this book the reader should be able to find their way around the drugs world with a reasonable degree of expertise.

- Secondly the book suggests ways in which you can spot the danger signs and recognise when a young person is using drugs or alcohol to excess. You will be able to do this by knowing what drugs and alcohol do to people and by applying that knowledge. Importantly, we will also make some suggestions as to what you might do if you find that a young person is abusing drugs or alcohol.

- In addition the book is also designed to enable adults and young people, to recognise that they may either have an existing problem or are prone towards developing a problem. We believe that it is possible to spot well in advance which types of people are particularly vulnerable to substance abuse or addiction. This is achieved through a 'risk factor' or 'odds ratio' approach which makes a person aware that they may be, say, five times as likely to develop a drink problem as George down the road given that they both drink the same amount. We will also suggest *why* a person is at risk.

There are two parts to this book and, although it is not actually divided up, all the chapters will fall into either *Background to substance use* or

Assessment of substance use. It is probably not strictly necessary to read all the chapters as some of them mainly contain information of general interest. It is suggested however that familiarity with these chapters will provide the reader with useful background knowledge that will help the reader not only to improve their communication skills in this area, but also to overcome substance abuse related problems as and when they arise.

Chapter 2 traces a brief history of drugs through the ages from 5,000 BC! This is useful in that it shows that drugs are not just a phenomenon which appeared in the 1960s. It is also actually quite interesting and may make you question many aspects of our current drugs policy.

In Chapter 3, although not strictly necessary, we give you accurate information about the various drugs and how they act on the body. We've obviously done our best to present the information in as palatable a manner as possible, but it is difficult to make psychopharmacology readable. This chapter is rather worrying too – particularly the part played by alcohol.

'Why do we take drugs?' Chapter 4 will not answer that question because science has yet to find out, but it will give you an insight into quite a few theories and will explain the author's own standpoint.

The extent of substance use is covered in Chapter 5. It is important to know who's using what within our society and this chapter gives details of some of the latest figures based on our own work as well as on the work of others. Figures may well not be as high as you have been led to believe.

The 'Risk Factors' are examined in Chapter 6 and we look at all those factors affecting substance use such as genetics, religious beliefs, family substance misuse and so on. We explain the influences which all these have on young people.

In Chapter 7 we take the knowledge gained in the previous chapter and explain how to apply it to your own situation.

Finally, in Chapter 8, we make some suggestions as to where you might go with the information you have gained.

Perspective

Where is this book coming from? The author was a psychologist carrying out research into substance abuse at a large UK university and as such the book was written from primarily a psychological perspective. However this does not mean that the topic will be confined to psychological theories from the likes of Sigmund Freud (who had a close affinity to cocaine anyway) or to those of Timothy Leary (Professor of Psychology in San Francisco, keen 1960s and

1970s advocate of LSD and latterly to be found permanently orbiting the globe in a custom made coffin). Psychology encompasses many disciplines from biology to sociology and this holistic perspective is particularly important when discussing substance use so we will not be sticking too rigidly to any one perspective.

Bearing this in mind the attitude taken will hopefully be one of realism and will look at the problem of substance abuse within the contexts of our society. In this way although the book is based on sound academic principals and theories supported by formal scientific research, these perspectives will be tempered by the realism of life in our modern world.

Terminology

Drugs

There are literally thousands of substances/drugs, which can have an effect on the human mind and body. Some of these we use daily (caffeine in tea and coffee for instance), others only occasionally (maybe champagne on special occasions). Still others are classified by governments as being illegal (marijuana) while we are encouraged by those same governments to use others (alcohol). Within the context of this book all these many different drugs will be treated as essentially the same – as psychotropic substances – or rather as substances which can have a profound effect on the way we act and behave.

In particular very little distinction will be drawn between alcohol and similar, but illegal, drugs. In other words, alcohol will be treated as the powerful drug it is. This book will not go into the pros and cons of the prohibition of marijuana and other drugs compared to the promotion of alcohol, and unless there are specific reasons not to do so, whenever the words 'drugs' or 'substances' are referred to, alcohol is generally to be included in that term.

Addiction

Addiction and its associated word '. . . holic' are two of the most difficult words in the English language to define. They are also two of the most misused. They are words that defy simple explanation and mean different things to different people.

Stereotyping can have a useful function, often as a defence mechanism, but unfortunately when it comes to the area of addiction, the stereotypical reaction to the phrase 'drug addict' often serves no useful function. At the most basic level the phrase may conjure up the image of an emaciated and dirty young person living in a sordid squat and sticking blunt and dirty needles directly into his jugular vein half a dozen times a day. Attached to the needle would be a syringe filled with heroin of dubious quality which had been sold to them by a person of Southern European or maybe Far Eastern origins who had originally hooked them on the drug while hanging around outside their college. If asked to elaborate a person may then go on to say that the drug addict, if male, pays for their habit by housebreaking and mugging old ladies or, if female, through prostitution.

The image that probably does not come to mind is that of the elderly lady who has been drinking a third of a bottle of sherry for years at the same time as popping pills for her 'nerves' and various sleeping pills at night. Equally the picture of the alcohol guzzling journalist who puts the stereotypical addict in our thoughts in the first place might also not spring immediately to mind, but they may be just as much an addict as the person mainlining heroin. (Or are we unfairly stereotyping when we describe journalists in this way?) As well, we are increasingly being bombarded with different types of 'holic'. The chocoholic and the sexholic are two that come to mind as having appeared in recent years in the media.

Two Polish psychologists described case studies of 'addiction' to carrots (carrotaholic?) and there have been numerous reports of addiction to exercise, particularly marathon running and aerobics, as well as addictions to peanut butter and addiction to ice-cream. Basically if you can think of something that brings pleasure to human beings someone else will have suggested that people can become addicted to it. We even came across a reference to 'Whopper Fever' a condition apparently experienced by addicts of hamburgers, although whether or not this violates the principal of humans becoming addicted to things that bring pleasure is open to some debate!

So this word 'addiction' has clearly lost its meaning and has been so popularised as to become largely irrelevant, but from a scientific standpoint and for the purposes of this book, how can the term be understood?

Firstly, does a substance or drug have to be involved if a person is to be classed as an addict? Probably not. There have been various pioneers who have shown that there is a serious case for saying that non-substance activities like gambling show all the characteristics of an addiction: but what are these characteristics? For the sake of argument we are going to classify an addiction as a condition, substance involving or not, where the following phenomena are found:

1. **Tolerance:** A person needs more and more of a substance or activity to achieve the desired effect.
2. **Withdrawal:** A person suffers mental or physical torments if the substance or activity is abruptly withdrawn.
3. **Salience:** The substance or activity is at the centre of a person's life. In other words, a significant proportion of a person's time is spent in indulging in the activity or in planning ways of indulging.
4. **Craving:** A person has an intense desire to use the substance or carry out the activity in spite of adverse consequences.

If these criteria are fulfilled then it seems likely that even if a person is not actually an addict, they at least have some form of significant problem. Even so, is it useful to talk about addiction, given the confusion surrounding its meaning? Probably not. If, as is contended by this book, substance use were normal and possibly not even particularly unhealthy then perhaps it would be more appropriate to think in terms of 'Use' and 'Abuse'.

Use versus abuse

Although it is a contentious and generally controversial thing to say, the use of mind-altering substances is a natural thing for humans to do. History supports this notion because, for whatever reasons, humans seem to feel the need to alter their state of consciousness and invariably do so at every given opportunity. To do this in a reasonable and controlled way may not be a particularly harmful thing to do (but more on that later), however when 'use' changes into 'abuse' then harm is caused.

What are the differences between use and abuse? Broadly the difference is not only a question of semantics, but of action too. In the context of this book then, we will go with the following definitions:

- **Use:** Any substance use that does not dramatically alter a person's lifestyle or place them at particular risk.
- **Abuse:** Substance use where a person's lifestyle is detrimentally altered by that use. This phrase 'detrimentally altered' can be used in a very broad sense and could equally well refer to adverse financial consequences as to medical and social problems.

Therefore the stance taken by this book is that substance use by the vast majority of humans is almost inevitable and not something to be too concerned about, but that this use can change to substance abuse which is both an abnormal and a dangerous behaviour.

The BioPsychoSocial approach

BioPsychoSocial (BPS) is quite possibly one of the worst words in the English language. However its meaning is at the heart of the current philosophy surrounding the causes of substance abuse and it is a term which will be used as a foundation concept in this book. Thankfully, it is not quite as appalling as it might first seem and it is important to clearly understand its meaning and the influence that this school of thought has on current substance abuse theory. The word can be broken down into three distinct parts:

1. **Bio**: This part of the word refers to the influence that genetics and brain biochemistry has over a person's susceptibility to substance abuse.
2. **Psycho**: The 'psycho' part of the model refers to psychological character-istics, aspects of personality if you like. For instance it has been shown that people who use various different substances tend to have lower self-esteem than people do who do not use. There are numerous other characteristics which appear to be common to substance abusers and this area will be discussed in some depth later.
3. **Social**: The final part of the word basically considers a person's surround-ings, their environment and the way they interact with, and are acted upon, by other people. It is also used as a catchall for anything which does not fit into the other two terms.

As we said, the BPS approach is at the heart of this book and the term will be used a great deal so it is important to understand its meaning. A full explanation of the BPS theories of substance abuse can be found towards the end of Chapter 4.

Conclusion

It has been accepted that people who abuse substances are different from people who simply use them. If this were not the case then everyone who has ever taken a drug would either be a substance abuser or a substance user. Clearly there are differences and it is the purpose of this book to try and tease out some of those differences and to show how a person may reasonably assess their risk of falling foul of abuse.

Throughout this book a BPS stance will be taken.

Additionally the position that substance use is relatively normal whereas substance abuse is not will be adopted.

Chapter 2

A Brief History of Substance Use and Abuse

Humans have been finding ways of altering their state of consciousness ever since life began. Quite why this may be the case is an intriguing question not covered in depth here. Having said that, by later discussing some of the risk factors involved and looking at ways of identifying why one person should be at risk from substance abuse rather than another, we may, in part and indirectly, answer this question. It remains though, that the reasons behind our fundamental desire to change the perception of the world are fascinating and complex. Is the world such a terrible place that we have to hide behind the effects of various different substances or is there some deep seated, primal and fundamental reason why we should have to drink ten pints of lager on a Friday night?

These questions will have to go largely unanswered, but it remains true that activities to alter consciousness have been common for a long time and in order to place current substance abuse in context it is instructive to consider the historical perspective. This chapter is not intended as an exhaustive review of drug use through the ages, but rather will trace some of the major events that have occurred since humans began to use drugs.

The first recorded reference to drug use is in 5,000 BC when the Sumarians were known to use opium. At around 3,500 BC the Egyptians are believed to have distilled alcohol for the first time and, about the same time, tea first started to be used by the ancient Chinese. It is thought that people, in what later became Switzerland, started to chew poppy seeds around 2,500 BC and in 1,500 BC the Chichimecs in Mexico ingested Psilocybin as part of their religious rituals. Interestingly, the first mention of addiction came in 300 BC when the Greek doctor Erasistratus warned of the addictive properties of opium.

From this period on, references can be found relating to alcohol, tea and opium in numerous places, but it is not until after the birth of Christ that another significant step is thought to have occurred. This was when cocoa cultivation first began in Peru at around 1208, where it was heralded as a gift from the Sun God by the Inca people and given divine status. At about this period, it is believed that the Chinese and other peoples of the Far East were widely using opium, a state that continued until 1729 when China prohibited the use or sale of opium.

In 1493, tobacco was first brought into Europe by Columbus when he returned from America and the habit of smoking quickly caught on. It was not popular with everyone however, and during the 17th century in Russia, Czar Michael Federovitch executed anyone caught with tobacco. About 1650 Sultan Murad of the Ottoman Empire hanged, beheaded, quartered and crushed anyone found in possession of tobacco.

In 1762 Thomas Dover developed Dover's Powders which he prescribed mainly for gout although it was widely used for many conditions over the next 150 years. Dover's Powders were essentially a tincture of opium similar to laudanum that had been used in America since about 1525.

Although cannabis had been used for many years outside Europe, it is particularly important to note that, in 1800, Napoleon's army, on its return from Egypt, introduced marijuana to Europe where it quickly caught on amongst the avant-garde community.

During the 19th century, in common with the Industrial Revolution, considerable steps were made in chemistry, and in 1805 morphine was isolated and described by the German chemist Friedrich Serturner; cocaine was also isolated in its pure form. It is interesting to note that in the same year it was isolated, Freud started to personally use cocaine and to prescribe it for the treatment of morphine addiction.

It was during this century that two Opium Wars took place between the British and the Chinese. Given current propaganda it seems intuitive to think that the British went to war to stop the Chinese from trading in opium when in point of fact it was actually the other way around. The Chinese had banned the opium trade in 1729 and the British were determined to see them carry on.

It is also during this century that fears, particularly in America, were growing about the dangers of alcohol and various temperance societies were formed. Throughout this period marijuana was grown as a cash crop all over North America where it was turned into rope, sails, linens, blankets, clothing and numerous other articles. It was considered so important that the early English settlers were ordered by James I to produce marijuana on a commercial basis and export it back to England.

In 1801 in America, federal tax on alcohol was abolished and in 1804 the Edinburgh based doctor Thomas Trotter wrote 'In medical language, I consider drunkenness, strictly speaking, to be a disease, produced by a remote cause, and giving birth to actions and movements in the living body that disorder the functions of health. The habit of drunkenness is a disease of the mind'.

The American Society for the Promotion of Temperance was founded in Boston in 1826 and seven years later there were 6,000 local branches with more than a million members and in 1840 Benjamin Parsons, an English clergyman, declared 'Alcohol stands pre-eminent as a destroyer. I never knew a person become insane who was not in the habit of taking a portion of alcohol everyday'. Parsons listed forty-two diseases caused by alcohol, among them inflammation of the brain, scrofula, mania, dropsy, nephritis and gout. He seems to have got it about right although he did miss one or two.

In 1884 Sigmund Freud treated his depression with cocaine, and reported feeling 'exhilaration and lasting euphoria, which in no way differs from the normal euphoria of the healthy person. You perceive an increase in self-control and possess more vitality and capacity for work. In other words you are simply normal, and it is soon hard to believe that you are under the influence of a drug'.

The report of the Royal Commission on Opium in 1885 concluded that opium was more like common alcohol than a substance to be feared and abhorred. Nine years later the Report of the Indian Hemp Drug Commission, which ran to over three thousand pages in seven volumes, was published. This inquiry, commissioned by the British government, concluded:

> There is no evidence of any weight regarding the mental and moral injuries from the moderate use of these drugs ... moderation does not lead to excess in hemp any more that it does in alcohol. Regular, moderate use of ganja or bhang produces the same effects as moderate and regular doses of whiskey.

The commission's proposal to tax bhang was never put into effect, in part, perhaps because one of the commissioners was Indian and cautioned that Moslem law and Hindu custom forbid 'taxing anything that gives pleasure to the poor'.

Norman Kerr, an English doctor and president of the British Society for the Study of Inebriety, declared in 1894 that 'Drunkenness has generally been regarded as a sin, a vice, or a crime. But there is now a consensus of intelligent opinion that habitual and periodic drunkenness is often either a symptom or sequel of disease. The victim can no more resist alcohol than any man with ague can resist shivering.'

Heroin was synthesised from morphine as a safe and non-addictive alternative in 1898. Two years later, James Daly wrote in the Boston Medical and Surgical Journal that heroin '. . . possesses many advantages over morphine . . . it is not hypnotic; and there is no danger of acquiring a habit.'

In 1901 the American Senate adopted a resolution, introduced by Henry Cabot Lodge, to forbid the sale by American traders of opium and alcohol 'to aboriginal tribes and uncivilised races'. These provisions were later extended to include 'uncivilised elements in America itself and in its territories, such as Indians, Alaskans, the inhabitants of Hawaii, railroad workers, and immigrants at ports of entry'. This less than wholly enlightened attitude was extended in 1902 when the Committee on the Acquirement of the Drug habit of the American Pharmaceutical Association declared 'If the Chinaman cannot get along without his dope, we can get along without him'.

Up until 1903 one of the 'secret' ingredients in Coca-Cola was cocaine, hence the name, but at that time the cocaine was taken out to be replaced by caffeine. Two years later the American temperance movement declared that their philosophy should include '. . . all poisonous substances which create unnatural appetite . . .' At the same time heroin was being marketed as a drug useful in weaning addicted persons off morphine, but at around the same time America banned the importing of opium. However, in 1910 it was reported in America that some large companies were giving cocaine free to their 'Negro' employees to encourage them to work harder but by 1914 Christopher Kochs wrote that 'most of the attacks upon white women of the South are the direct result of the cocaine crazed "Negro" brain. "Negro" cocaine fiends are now a known Southern menace'.

In 1912 the first 'stepping stones' or 'gateway' theory of substance abuse was described in America when it was written in *Century* magazine that:

> . . . *the relation of tobacco, especially in the form of cigarettes, and alcohol and opium is a very close one . . . Morphine is the legitimate consequence of alcohol, and alcohol is the legitimate consequence of tobacco. Cigarettes, drink, opium, is the logical and regular series.*

At the same time when promoting the prohibition amendment to the Constitution of America one congressman asserted that 'liquor will actually make a brute out of a Negro, causing him to commit unnatural crimes. The effect is the same on the white man, though the white man being further evolved, it takes a longer time to reduce him to the same level'.

At around this time it was estimated that in America tax on alcohol provided between half and two thirds of the state's income.

In 1920 the US Department of Agriculture published a pamphlet urging Americans to grow cannabis as a profitable undertaking.

Between 1920 and 1933 the use of alcohol was prohibited in the United States. In 1932 alone, approximately 45,000 persons received jail sentences for alcohol offences. During the first eleven years of the Volstead Act, 17,971 persons were appointed to the Prohibition Bureau. 11,982 were terminated 'without prejudice', and 1,604 were dismissed for bribery, extortion, theft, falsification of records, conspiracy, forgery, and perjury. By 1928 it was estimated that doctors were making an estimated $40,000,000 annually by writing prescriptions for whisky as a medicine.

In 1921 cigarettes were made illegal in fourteen states in America, and ninety-two anti-cigarette bills were pending in a further twenty-eight states. Young women, but not men, were expelled from universities for smoking cigarettes.

In 1924 the manufacture of heroin was prohibited in the United States of America.

During a nationwide radio broadcast in 1928 entitled *The Struggle of Mankind Against Its Deadliest Foe*, celebrating the second annual Narcotic Education Week, Richmond Hobson, prohibition crusader and anti-narcotics propagandist, declared:

> *Suppose it were announced that there were more than a million lepers among our people. Think what a shock the announcement would produce! Yet drug addiction is far more incurable than leprosy, far more tragic to its victims, and is spreading like a moral and physical scourge . . . Most of the daylight robberies, daring hold-ups, cruel murders and similar crimes of violence are now known to be committed chiefly by drug addicts, who constitute the primary cause of our alarming crime wave. Drug addiction is more communicable and less curable than leprosy . . . Upon the issue hangs the perpetuation of civilisation, the destiny of the world, and the future of the human race.*

By 1928, morphine was being widely used in Europe and it was estimated that one per cent of Germany's doctors were morphine addicts and in 1935 the American Medical Association passed a resolution declaring that 'alcoholics are valid patients'. In 1936 the Pan-American Coffee Bureau was organised to promote coffee use in the US and between 1938 and 1941 coffee consumption increased 20 per cent.

Shortly before the Marijuana Tax Act came into force in 1937, Commissioner Harry J Anslinger wrote: 'How many murders, suicides, robberies, criminal assaults, hold-ups, burglaries and deeds of maniacal insanity marijuana causes each year, especially among the young, can only be conjectured'. A year later Albert Hoffman stumbled across LSD.

In 1941 Chiang Kai-Shek ordered the complete suppression of the poppy; laws were enacted providing the death penalty for anyone guilty of cultivating the poppy, manufacturing opium, or offering it for sale whilst at about the same time the editor of the American medical journal the *Military Surgeon*, declared in an editorial entitled The Marijuana Bugaboo that:

> . . . *the smoking of the leaves, flowers, and seeds of Cannabis sativa is no more harmful than the smoking of tobacco . . . It is hoped that no witch hunt will be instituted in the military service over a problem that does not exist.*

Ludwig von Mises, a leading modern free-market economist and social philosopher, wrote in 1949:

> *Opium and morphine are certainly dangerous habit-forming drugs, but once the principle is admitted that it is the duty of governments to protect the individual against his own foolishness, no serious objections can be advanced against further encroachments. A good case could be made out in favour of the prohibition of alcohol and nicotine. And why limit the government's benevolent providence to the protection of the individual's body only? Is not the harm a man can inflict on his mind and soul even more disastrous than any bodily evils? Why not prevent him from reading books and seeing bad plays, from looking at bad paintings and statues and listening to bad music? The mischief done by bad ideologies, surely, is much more pernicious, both for the individual and for the whole society, than that done by narcotic drugs.*

Two years later the United Nations estimated that there were approximately 200 million marijuana users in the world, the major places being India, Egypt, North Africa, Mexico, and the United States, and in 1954 three quarters of the French people questioned about wine asserted that wine is 'good for one's health', and one quarter held that it is 'indispensable'. It was estimated that a third of the electorate in France received all or part of its income from the production or sale of alcoholic beverages; and that there was one alcohol outlet for every forty-five inhabitants.

In 1955 the Shah of Iran prohibited the cultivation and use of opium, used in the country for thousands of years. This ban produced a flourishing illicit market in opium. In 1969 the prohibition was lifted, opium growing was resumed under state inspection, and more than 110,000 persons received opium from physicians and pharmacies as 'registered addicts'. In America in 1956 the Narcotics Control Act was enacted; it provided the death penalty for the sale of heroin to a person under eighteen by one over eighteen.

It was noted that in 1958 ten per cent of the arable land in Italy was under viticulture with two million people earning their living wholly or partly from the production or sale of wine.

The United States report to the United Nations Commission on Narcotic Drugs for 1960 reported that on December 31st of that year there were 44,906 addicts in the United States.

In 1963 tobacco sales in America were estimated at $8.1 billion of which $3.3 billion went to the government in taxes and three years later Senator Warren Magnuson, sponsored by the American Agriculture Department went on a travelogue to promote cigarette consumption overseas, particularly in the Far East.

America's 'War on Drugs', which continues to this day, began in 1967. In the same year the tobacco industry in the United States spent an estimated $250 million on advertising cigarette smoking. A year later the US tobacco industry had gross sales of $8 billion with 544 billion cigarettes being smoked that year.

In 1968 Canadians bought almost three billion aspirin tablets and approximately 56 million standard doses of amphetamines. In that same year it was estimated that six to seven per cent of all prescriptions written in the UK were for barbiturates and that about 500,000 people in the UK were regular users.

President Nixon declared in 1971 that 'America's Public Enemy No.1 is drug abuse' and at the same time Turkey banned cultivation of the opium poppy. A year later the American Bureau of Narcotics estimated that there were 560,000 drug addicts in the USA and allocated $1 billion in a three year attack on the drugs trade.

Since 1971 the world's drug policy has been largely influenced by that of the United States of America which, as we have seen, has itself a tortured history when it comes to drug misuse. Their policies appear to be tied up with many fundamental Christian beliefs and with the belief that they should act as the world's police force. In many instances America's attitude towards drug use is contradictory with the degree of harmfulness of a drug bearing no relationship to illegality or otherwise. Indeed the opposite appears to be true in many instances with successive United States governments supporting tobacco farmers and alcohol producers.

America's declared 'War on Drugs' has been going on for a considerable length of time and has been largely echoed around the world, but its effectiveness has been dubious and the cost high. It has been estimated that between 1986 and 1991 this war has cost $35 billion in the States alone. Whatever the merits or otherwise of the War on Drugs, its influence around the world has been tremendous. The aim was to end casual drug use. It was felt that the best way to get casual use to end was to put the primary focus on demand from within America, rather than putting the major focus on the supply from other nations.

Initially War on Drugs did appear to produce results. The biggest success was a reported 22 per cent decrease in cocaine use. However, it is not entirely clear that the War on Drugs was responsible. The middle class may have finally opened their eyes to the effects of cocaine usage. It is fair to assume that when a drug is first introduced, people have not yet seen the negative effects first hand, but, as time goes on, people see these effects, and begin to stay away from it. The War on Drugs, however, did nothing to curb drug usage among the poor. In fact, the opposite happened. Poor people used more cocaine, heroin and crack by 1992 than when the War on Drugs began.

One criticism of the War on Drugs was also the noticeable lack of focus on treatment and research. In 1989, only $925 million was allotted for treatment. Congress felt that this was so inadequate that it added $1.1 billion for treatment, prevention, and education. By 1992, the amount for treatment alone had grown to $1.9 billion.

As part of the War on Drugs, persons convicted of addiction related offences were often given the choice of a prison sentence or entry into a treatment programme. However, the offenders often preferred to serve out a prison term than go into treatment, possibly because the prison sentences were so much shorter than any treatment programme.

The US Bureau of Justice Statistics (1994) stated that in 1993 1.5 million Americans were in prison for felony offences. Of these 59.6 per cent or 894,000 persons were in prison for drug related offences. Out of the remaining 606,000 prisoners 50 per cent reported being under the influence of alcohol or other drugs when they committed their crimes. These proportions are similar in the UK.

This brief history of world drug use shows that substance use has had a roller-coaster ride through the ages. Finally, to illustrate this point, two extreme examples are the actions of the Sultan Murad IV of the Ottoman Empire on the one hand who back in the Middle Ages beheaded, hanged, quartered and crushed anyone found smoking tobacco compared with the attitude of the United States government in 1920 when the Department of Agriculture published a monograph urging the Americans to grow cannabis as a profitable undertaking.

Alongside the question posed earlier as to why humans feel it important to alter their state of consciousness is the question of why governments and rulers of all political hues feel it is important to stop them. This question opens the door to a largely philosophical debate that would be best covered elsewhere, but it is interesting to wonder exactly why it is that, for instance, the American government, feels the need to spend tens of billions of dollars on stopping an activity which has been going on in one form or another since the dawn of time.

Numerous questions might be posed and solutions offered, but so far no one has been able to satisfactorily explain what motivates governments to behave in this way. The knee jerk response is, of course, to say that drugs are dangerous and that the government is protecting its subjects from themselves, but given the inconsistencies in the policies over the years, this does not seem to be a particularly strong argument.

The conclusion is clearly that the world's policy regarding substance misuse is in turmoil and has been throughout the ages, that these policies are constantly changing and that there is little consistency or logic to many of the rules and regulations which govern substance misuse.

Chapter 3

Drugs: Their Actions and Effects

It is important to present as much detail of the background of substances of abuse as practical because without it everything else in the book is something of an abstraction. For instance if we were writing a book on the dangers of scuba diving it would be rather hard for the reader to imagine the bends if they had never seen the sea, either personally or on television, and had no concept of water. In a similar way, it is hard to understand about risks from substance of abuse if we do not know anything about substances themselves.

Unfortunately, a lot of this background is rather dry as it is not particularly easy to make a description of the post-synaptic cleft (or whatever) especially exciting. This is not a chapter on heavy pharmacology, but it does give some of the technical details of how drugs work when taken by people.

We have divided this chapter up into small sections and it is suggested that the reader looks at the first three sections which deal with general topics and then move onto the sections dealing with the specific substances or substance groups they are interested in.

The chapter contains the following sections:
- What is a drug?
- Acute mechanisms.
- Chronic mechanisms.

We then look at alcohol and alcoholism, followed by sections on the actions of cannabis, amphetamines (speed), cocaine, the opiates (heroin and others), hallucinogens (LSD, Ecstasy), along with phencyclidine (Angel Dust).

Inhalants and a discussion on benzodiazepines (Valium and Temazepam) round off this section.

What is a Drug?

It may appear sufficient to say that a drug is something prescribed by a doctor or bought over the counter at a pharmacy, but what about alcohol or solvents, are they not drugs too? In the same context, could not certain substances found in food such as salt, glucose or vitamins also be considered to be drugs? If a certain foodstuff is eaten primarily for sustenance then clearly it is not a drug, but if that foodstuff is high in glucose and is deliberately given to a diabetic in hypoglycaemic shock is it not then a drug?

If this type of reasoning is adopted, it is fair to say that a substance may or may not be a drug depending upon the context in which it is used. In other words, it is the intent which is the determining factor in defining if a substance is a drug.

Therefore, a drug may be any substance, both manufactured and naturally occurring, that is used primarily to bring about psychological, physiological or biochemical change in a person.

Acute, Short Term Actions

Drugs of abuse alter the brain's normal balance and level of biochemical activity. In order to have these effects, a drug must first reach the brain. This is accomplished by the drug diffusing from the circulatory system into the brain. The routes of administration, methods by which a drug enters the bloodstream, affect how quickly a drug penetrates the brain. Additionally, the chemical structure of a drug plays an important role in the ability of a drug to cross from the circulatory system into the brain. The four main routes of administration for drugs of abuse are:

- **Oral:** By mouth, e.g. tablets.
- **Nasal:** Snorting up the nose, e.g. cocaine.
- **Injection:** Directly into a vein or a muscle or just under the skin, e.g. heroin.
- **Inhalation:** Smoking, e.g. cannabis.

There is a fifth method which for some reason is much favoured by the French and that is getting a drug into your system via a suppository inserted into the back passage. This can result in very rapid onset of drug action and can be helpful if, for instance, an epileptic is having a particularly bad fit, but it is not recommended as a general rule.

Interestingly, different primary routes of administration are favoured by different countries. As noted, the French prefer the anal route while the British and Americans favour oral ingestion and the Spanish and other Southern Mediterranean countries prefer giving just about everything by injection.

When taken orally, the drug must be absorbed by the stomach or gut which results in a delay before effects become apparent. When the nasal route of administration is used, as is often the case for cocaine, effects are usually felt within a couple of minutes, as the capillary rich mucous membranes of the nose rapidly absorb into the bloodstream. Intravenous injection administration usually produces effects in about fifteen seconds to two minutes and is slowed only by the detour back through the lungs that the blood must take to reach the brain. Lastly, the inhalation method bypasses the veins system completely because the drug is absorbed into the pulmonary circulation which goes directly from the lungs to the heart and then to the brain. As a result, effects can be felt within five to ten seconds, making inhalation the fastest route of administration. The route of administration can determine the drug's potency and the efficacy of the drug on the brain's activity, thereby contributing to the abuse potential of the drug.

Distinct from other psychoactive agents, drugs of abuse, in part, affect those areas of the brain involved with feelings of pleasure and reward. Positive sensations experienced during these activities are mediated by the brain's reward system. Studies have shown that direct stimulation of the reward system can produce extreme pleasure that encourages people to continually seek to re-experience that pleasure. Animals with electrodes implanted in these areas will repeatedly press a bar, or do any other required task, to receive electrical stimulation to these pleasure zones. The fact that animals will forego food and drink or will willingly experience a painful stimulus to receive stimulation of the reward system attests to the powerful reinforcing characteristics of the reward system. Some animals will even starve themselves to death in order to receive this intense pleasure.

Most drugs of abuse, either directly or indirectly, are presumed to affect this brain reward system. If animals will starve themselves to death at the same time as receiving pain just to have this area stimulated, can you imagine what humans might go through to get similar sensations? Look at the sacrifices some people make to achieve orgasm, a fleeting sensation lasting a few seconds. If drugs work in a similar area of the pleasure centres and produce similar feelings that last for hours then humans are likely to go through hell to seek them out.

While growing evidence suggests that the brain reward system plays a role in the reinforcing properties of most drugs of abuse, the precise mechanisms involved are complex, vary among substances, and have yet to be completely described. Information on this area is becoming increasingly complex as our knowledge base grows. Suffice it to say that drugs of abuse stimulate the pleasure centres of the brain and that this stimulation can be so strong that people will do just about anything to re-experience that sensation once it has been sampled.

Chronic, Long Term Actions

This short section looks at the long term *actions* of substances of abuse, not the long term *effects* which are quite different things.

Chronic, long term exposure to drugs of abuse can cause changes in the brain that may take weeks, months, and possibly years to reverse once drug use has stopped.

Most drugs of abuse have complex actions in the central nervous system (CNS) and other parts of the body resulting in a variety of behavioural effects. In general, tolerance develops to many of the effects of drug abuse and a withdrawal syndrome occurs on cessation after prolonged use. However, the details of these phenomena vary from drug to drug, and the specific details of the biological mechanisms that underlie these phenomena are not completely understood. They are, fortunately, not crucial to this book.

As mentioned, tolerance to a drug is the phenomenon by which more of the drug is required to produce a given effect. This response occurs with many types of drugs. It is a common characteristic of several drugs that while tolerance develops to some of the effects, sensitisation can also occur to some of the others. Sensitisation is the opposite of tolerance and occurs when the effects of a given dose of a drug increase after repeated, but intermittent, administration. Sensitisation to a drug's effects can play a significant role in supporting drug taking behaviour with one of the commonest examples of this phenomenon being cannabis. Often a person has difficulty in getting stoned the first few times, but after that it becomes easier and easier. This may be in part due to the fact that a new user may not be a tobacco smoker and so has to learn to inhale, but it is also a fact that can occur years later, even if a person has not used the drug for a decade. 'A quarter of a spliff and they're off again'. We don't really know why this happens.

Dependence may be described as a type of neuroadaptation to drug exposure. With prolonged use of a drug, cells in the brain adapt to its presence such that the drug is required to maintain normal cell function. On abrupt withdrawal of the drug, the cell behaves abnormally and a withdrawal syndrome ensues. Generally, the withdrawal syndrome is characterised by a series of signs and symptoms that are opposite to those of the drug's acute effects. For example, withdrawal of sedative drugs produce excitation and irritability. Conversely, withdrawal of stimulants produces profound depression.

The magnitude of the withdrawal syndrome varies from drug to drug. Although the severity varies, withdrawal is associated with the cessation of use of most drugs of abuse. Opiates, cocaine, amphetamines, barbiturates, alcohol, and benzodiazepines produce pronounced and sometimes severe withdrawal symptoms (to the extent of being causal in the onset of epileptic type fits in the case of benzodiazepines which, in turn, can lead to death), while those for nicotine and caffeine are less intense. A mild withdrawal episode is associated with discontinued cannabis use, while there is none at all associated with LSD. No matter the severity of the physical withdrawal syndrome, its existence can create a craving or desire for the drug and dependence can play a very strong role in recurrent patterns of relapse and maintaining drug-seeking behaviour to forestall withdrawal.

At one time, withdrawal was believed to peak within several hours after drug taking stopped and, similarly, common knowledge held that tolerance to most drugs was thought to dissipate gradually with time as the brain readapted to the drug's disappearance. It now appears that persistent, residual neuroadaptation may be present, which can last for months or possibly years, and may be associated with the pathways that mediate physical dependence. An important component of this phenomenon may be the learning which takes place during drug-taking behaviour. Moreover, with repeated cycles of abstinence and re-initiation of drug use, the time required to elicit drug dependence grows shorter and shorter.

The data indicates the existence of long-lasting, drug induced neuroadaptive changes that persist for as yet undefined periods of time. Although information explaining this effect is lacking, these changes may help account for the relapses that sometimes occur in long term abstinent, drug-dependant individuals.

The next part of the chapter moves onto specific drugs and drug groups.

Alcohol

With the exception of caffeine, alcohol (ethyl alcohol or ethanol) is the most widely used drug of abuse in the world. For this reason and also because of its place in society, the substance will be discussed in some depth, but please note that this discussion is by no means exhaustive and merely skims the surface of this topic. In presenting this, we have attempted to ensure that only facts relevant to this book's topic areas are covered.

Alcohol is a general non-selective central nervous system depressant and is quite probably the source of more individual and general social problems than the rest of the abused drugs put together.

Alcohol is a simple molecule which is soluble in both water and fat and which readily passes through human membranes. It is rapidly and completely absorbed through the entire gastro intestinal tract and quickly crosses the blood-brain barrier with up to 90 per cent crossing into the brain almost immediately after it is drunk.

Following absorption, alcohol is metabolised by the liver and stomach and this occurs independently of the amount of alcohol that has been consumed and is strictly related to time. Alcohol is excreted at the rate of 10 millilitres of 100 per cent ethanol per hour and there is very little an individual can do to speed this process up. Even in severe alcohol poisoning the slow steady metabolism by the liver is the only way that a person can be effectively detoxified. There is no known way to speed up this process so if you have 50 millilitres of alcohol in your system it will take 5 hours to break down. This is a simple fact, but one that is often forgotten by drivers the morning after a big night out.

In common with all depressant drugs, alcohol acts globally on all neurones of the brain producing disorientation, impaired memory and an unstable effect except opiates and opiodes which work on specific receptors.

Alcoholism

Alcoholism shows a tendency to run in families with one third of alcoholics having had at least one parent who was alcoholic. Adoption studies in the USA and Scandinavia have shown that sons of alcoholics are three to four times more likely to be alcoholic than sons of non-alcoholics without regard to who raised them.

There has been some suggestion that there are types of alcoholics; Type 1 and Type 2. Type 1, which occurs in both sexes, is usually not severe and is associated with mild adult onset alcohol abuse. For Type 2, which occurs only in men and is extremely severe and life threatening, and accounts for 25 per cent of all alcoholics, it is necessary to have a father who had teenage onset severe alcoholism associated with serious criminality.

Leaving genetics aside, people are more likely to become alcoholics if they metabolise alcohol in a certain way. For example, people from the Far East often have a low tolerance to alcohol and very few are alcoholics. For various reasons involving enzymes they tend to get drunk really easily and suffer from the most dreadful hangovers, which are prime reasons for them not to drink too much. At present there is a good deal of research interest in the possibility of a genetic variation in the enzymes which control alcohol metabolism. Most people with high tolerance are more at risk of developing alcoholism.

Mode of action

In a similar way to some sedative drugs, alcohol suppresses all the neurones in the brain producing disorientation, mental clouding, amnesia and decreased judgement. It is thought to work, at least in part, by a process known as membrane fluidisation. This is where alcohol dissolves the cell membrane, enters the cell and distorts its anatomy. The degree of intoxication can be positively correlated with the degree of cell membrane fluidisation. The distortion of the fluidised membranes reduces the efficiency of the method by which the brain cells communicate.

Principally alcohol has the effect of being a non-selective central nervous system depressant, although it can also suppress respiratory functions which can be the cause of death with alcohol overdose. It is also anti-convulsant, but there can be a rebound effect and if an epileptic alcoholic suddenly stops drinking there may be an increased risk of convulsion.

There is a compound effect with certain drugs mainly within the benzodiazepine family of drugs (valium and so on) and if both alcohol and benzodiazepines are taken at the same time each has an effect on the other and the risk of respiratory failure and other problems is increased.

Alcohol also dilates blood vessels to the skin and this can lead to a decrease in body temperature. This means that you should never give alcohol to people suffering from hypothermia.

Detrimental effects of alcohol

Many people know that alcohol has a severe, long-term, irreversible effect on the liver, changing both its function and its physiology. 75 per cent of all alcohol related deaths are caused by liver cirrhosis, but it is not so widely known that alcohol causes many other problems too.

Short term psychological effects of alcohol are restricted to the central nervous system. At low doses it is unpredictable but may take the form of someone becoming an extrovert, being euphoric or possibly violent and aggressive. These behavioural changes are often due to a person's mood when they begin their drinking session and the setting in which they are doing their drinking. As the dose gets higher these social cues are of less importance as the sedative effects of alcohol increases and behavioural activity decreases.

With high doses of alcohol, hallucinations, delusions and talking too much are possible. Long term high usage may cause a chronic brain syndrome known as Korsakoff's Syndrome which may be similar in symptoms to senile dementia. Karsakoff's only resembles dementia in later stages (Wienke's is the late stage). People confabulate fantastical stories in Karsakoffs to 'infill' memory loss. Prolonged high usage may also increase the risk a person has of contracting tongue, mouth, throat and liver cancer. Alcohol may also promote tumour growth.

Some of the major adverse psychological and physiological changes brought about by alcohol uses are:

- **Liver disease**: There are three different types of this condition; Fatty Liver Disease which is not particularly dangerous and mainly causes some degree of pain in the right abdomen; Alcoholic Hepatitis is characterised by liver cell neurosis and inflammatory change and presents with jaundice, increased temperature and pain. Cirrhosis is similar, but is normally terminal and is characterised by permanent structural damage to the liver.
- **General gastro-intestinal disorders**: Acute pancreatitis presents with mild abdominal pain and occasionally, with hypertension and renal failure. Chronic pancreatitis follows unremitting daily drinking for about ten years and is often diagnosed following complaints of chronic abdominal pain and weight loss. Pancreatic cancer is strongly associated with heavy drinking as is colonic or rectal cancer.

  Gastric and peptic ulcers are fairly common and are basically caused by increased acidity due to the alcohol. This may lead to holes in the stomach (duodenum) or the oesophagus.
- **Cardiovascular diseases**: Alcoholic cardiomyopathy occurs typically in middle-aged male beer drinkers and has all the usual signs and symptoms of chronic cardiac failure. Systemic hypertension is also not uncommon.
- **Haematological disorders**: Alcohol is also a bone marrow toxin.
- **Neurological disorders**: Alcohol-related fits occur during withdrawal and resemble classic tonic-clonic fits normally found in epilepsy.
- **Delirium tremens**: These generally first start to appear about 2–4 days after abstinence begins. Common symptoms include acute anxiety, sleeplessness, tremor, heart beat racing and increased perspiration. These symptoms are generally followed by disorientation, a fluctuating level of awareness, hallucinations, misperceptions, autonomic overactivity and intense fear. Hallucinations can be visual in which case they often consist of animals or insects (this is the 'amusing' pink elephant syndrome often mentioned in films). They can also be auditory which can be paranoid in nature. Sufferers may also have hallucinations when they feel things crawling over their skin. Liver damage is usually present in 90 per cent of these cases.

- **Alcoholic blackouts**: These are said to take three forms: state-dependant blackouts where the subject commonly hides money or drink and can only find these things when drunk again; fragmentary blackouts where the subject has no clear idea of when the blackouts started or finished and where there are often small 'islets' of intact memory; en bloc blackouts where the subject has a very clear idea of when the blackout started. This state may last from hours to days and often consists of the subject coming out of it in a strange place and not remembering how they got there. Three possible predictors of these blackouts are:
  – An early onset of drinking habits.
  – High peak levels of alcohol.
  – A past history of frequent head trauma.
- **Wernicke's Encephalopathy**: Primarily results from a vitamin deficiency and presents with opthalmoplegia, nystagmus, ataxia and confusion.
- **Coarsening of personality**: This is seen in chronic alcoholics and can consist of a loss of social skills, loss of inhibitions, a tendency to be irritable with facile jocularity and abusiveness. This is not always at time of acute intoxication.
- **Cognitive impairment**: Mild to moderate cognitive impairment has been found in chronic alcoholics, particularly with short term memory tasks and generalised IQ functioning. However, there is some indication that after abstinence of five years from alcohol some improvement is made. Many alcoholics have been found to have enlarged ventricles and a poor cerebral blood supply which hinder higher brain functions.
- **Musculoskeletal disorders**: Osteoporosis is made worse by alcohol as is gout which is caused by a build up of uric acid.
- **Endocrine disorders**: These may show as a bloated face, obesity and hypertension or impotence in men and poor fertility in women.
- **Metabolic disorders**: These are numerous and include: alcohol induced lactic acidosos, alcoholic ketacidosis, hyperlipidaema which is found in over a third of alcoholics, alcohol induced hypoglycaemia, and generalised disturbances in electrolyte and acid bases balances.

A black picture of alcohol has been painted here, but like many other drugs, these conditions tend only to result after prolonged and persistent abuse. However, we are not scaremongering, these conditions are all too common and we have dwelt on them at some length because so many people in the western world drink way in excess of safe levels.

Finally, what might be an interesting exercise would be to develop a fictitious drug with an imaginary name and attribute to it all of the above conditions, not to mention its tendency to promote violence, be involved in crime and so on and see if the authorities thought it ought to be heavily promoted through the media as alcohol is or banned . . .!

Cannabis

(marijuana, grass, dope, pot, weed, hash, gear, wacky backy)

Cannabis is the most widely used of the illegal drugs, probably on a scale similar to that of alcohol which is, of course, legal. Because its use is so commonplace and because there is much debate about whether it leads people to use hard drugs it is worthwhile discussing it in some depth.

What is it?

It is a psychoactive drug and thus may be classified as an hallucinogen. The various forms of cannabis mostly come from the plants *Cannabis sativa* and *Cannabis indica*, which grow throughout the world. It is available in three main forms:

- As a dried herb (composed of top leaves and buds – usually known as marijuana or grass).
- As a resin (usually known as hash or hashish), which is extracted from the buds and the flower heads in the country of origin.
- Less commonly as a sticky liquid (hash oil) which is prepared from the resin.

Herbal cannabis or grass is slowly gaining a greater market share. On a practical level grass is much harder to smuggle due to its bulk and aroma. Traditionally imported from Africa, Asia and the Caribbean, herbal cannabis is increasingly being 'home grown' in the UK and Europe.

Cannabis resin found in the UK comes from a variety of sources, traditionally the Indian subcontinent, Lebanon and Morocco, all of which differ considerably in colour, texture and aroma. Most resin turning up on the streets will have been reformulated in Europe and the different types will have different names such as 'red seal', 'rocky', 'slate', and many more.

History

The earliest record of cannabis use is from a compendium of medicines which was compiled for the Chinese emperor Shen Nung in about 2727BC. Since then the cannabis plant has been used for everything from making rope and cloth to its many medicinal purposes. Worldwide, it has been used medically for centuries and in the UK it is used illegally as an effective reliever of the symptoms of multiple sclerosis, hypoglycaemia and in certain instances, as a medication for the terminally ill.

The use of cannabis for its psychoactive (intoxicating) effect has always been a political issue. In the UK, cannabis was first used by young West Indian immigrants and by people who went to fashionable Soho jazz clubs during the 1950s. In the 1960s along with the hippy culture came the availability of cannabis to a wide range of young people. The use of the drug declined slightly in the 1970s, but with the dance scene kicking off in the 1980s with acid house, ravers, party goers and clubbers found it the perfect drug to bring them down and chill out after a hard night's dancing.

Relatively recent statistics (in 2000) in the UK showed that of 42,000 recorded drug offences each year, around 40,000 of these were related to cannabis possession. The legal costs and manpower requirements involved seemed disproportionate to the known effects of cannabis and in the UK recently the government re-categorised cannabis as a class C drug.

Previously negative attitudes towards cannabis have begun to soften. This in turn has resulted in a more relaxed attitude over its perceived effects. In part this may be due to the focus on its legal therapeutic uses. Some of these include relief of the symptoms of glaucoma and multiple sclerosis and relief of nausea. Research continues into the beneficial nature of the substance.

How is it used?

Cannabis is most commonly smoked. It is usually mixed with tobacco and rolled up with cigarette papers into a cannabis cigarette (often called a 'spliff', 'joint', 'reefer', or 'jay'). However it can also be smoked with or without tobacco in various forms of pipes and smoking devices (such as 'bongs' and 'water pipes'). Nowadays the smoking of cannabis through pipes (often using water to cool the smoke) has become more prevalent due to its greater efficiency. In cultures where cannabis is predominant such as the Caribbean it is most commonly smoked neat. This method is safer since it avoids problems associated with tobacco smoking.

Cannabis can also be eaten on its own or mixed in with recipes such as cakes, biscuits (hence 'hash cookies') or hot drinks as a form of tea. Eating it means that the active ingredients have to be absorbed through the stomach contents before entering the blood. This appears to be less efficient (therefore the user gets less 'value for money' and the dosage is less controllable). A smoker of cannabis can stop smoking once the required level of intoxication is reached whereas an eater will have difficulty in achieving what they feel is the right dosage.

The effects

The primary active ingredient is delta9-tetrahydrocannabinol (THC). Street marijuana contains typically about 15 per cent THC. Not everyone gets much effect from cannabis. Smoking cannabis produces fairly instant intoxication, the effects lasting from 1–4 hours depending on the amount used.

The most common and desired effects are:

- relaxation
- talkativeness
- cheerfulness and sense of well-being
- greater appreciation of sound and colour
- enhanced performance for tasks involving creativity

Undesirable effects include:

- loss of coordination
- loss of concentration
- dry mouth
- binge eating (known as the 'munchies')
- mild hallucinations
- sensory distortions
- mild panic and paranoia
- nausea and vomiting particularly when used with alcohol

There have been no recorded deaths from cannabis use and overdosage is rare. The 'morning after the night before' effect is far less strong than a hang-over from drinking alcohol. Driving whilst under the influence of cannabis can be dangerous, although the rashness and aggression displayed by drink drivers is unlikely to be present. The person may also not cross roads nor operate machinery safely.

The dangers

There are now many people in the UK who have used cannabis regularly or occasionally for at least 20 years, yet there is no conclusive evidence that long term use causes lasting damage to physical or mental health. Short term memory loss is reported by some users, however the main health problems stem from the method of use. Smoking any substance over a long period of time is a bad idea and frequent breathing in of cannabis smoke can lead to bronchitis and other respiratory disorders, not least cancer. The cannabis leaf contains much the same chemicals as tobacco, and a fresh cannabis smoke may contain as much tar as 20 cigarettes. Tar is associated with cancers of the mouth, throat and lung in cigarette smokers. In pipe smokers, tar is associated with cancer of the lips, gums and throat. With those who chew tobacco, tar is particularly associated with cancer of jaw, tongue and gums.

Whilst cannabis alone does not produce a physical dependency, psychological dependency occurs in about 10 per cent of users. Mixing it with tobacco will almost certainly cause a nicotine addiction in quite a short period of time. This is particularly undesirable in pregnancy, where it can damage not only the development of the foetus, but also the learning ability of the child. Regular smokers of cannabis also face the same risks of heart disease, cancer, respiratory and circulatory problems as do tobacco smokers. High-use cannabis smokers often develop bloodshot eyes, caused by the dilation of blood vessels. There may also be an increased risk of mental health problems in users who have a family history of psychosis.

Most psychoactive drugs have both positive and negative effects. People clearly use drugs because of the positive effects but don't always know, or choose to overlook, the negative. It is therefore the ratio of positive to negative effects that fuels much of the drugs debate. One of the negative effects concerns the theory that cannabis use leads to hard drug use.

The stepping stone versus the gateway theory

The former suggests that progression from the so-called 'soft' drugs such as cannabis to so-called 'hard' drugs such as heroin or cocaine is inevitable. While it is true that many of those who become heroin addicts have used cannabis first, the vast majority of people in the UK (and elsewhere) have never used so-called harder drugs. This would suggest that progression from cannabis is in fact, relatively rare.

The latter theory draws on the metaphor of a series of gates through which a user may pass. Each gateway leads to a different drug and new risks. Many hard drug users have followed a similar path from tobacco and alcohol to cannabis, to heroin and cocaine. Clearly, not everyone who likes an alcoholic drink ends up as a cocaine addict, but very few users of hard drugs have not tried cannabis first.

In reality the gateway theory seems to be far more credible. Recent research (2002) by the Home Office also concluded that 'the association between more harmful and less harmful drugs found in survey data is spurious' and that it is also likely that the gateway effects are 'very small'. However, the reason why young cannabis users are more likely to progress to harder drugs has provoked fierce debate – but a new study of twins (2003) has ruled out a strong genetic component. Researchers looked at over 300 pairs of same sex twins, identical and non-identical, in which one twin started using cannabis before the age of 17 and the other did not. Michael Lynskey and his team at Washington University School of Medicine found that the earlier user was two to five times more likely to go on to use harder drugs or become dependent on alcohol – regardless of whether they were an identical twin or not. The fact that identical twins, who share all of their genes, did not differ from non-identical twins, who share half, suggests that the progression is not the product of genes.

This study not only rules out a large genetic component but it also suggests that the home and the womb environment may not be a key factor either. However, Lynskey acknowledges that it is impossible to eliminate all nurture differences between twins. For example, one twin may have suffered a traumatic event in childhood that did not affect the other.

Denise Kandel at Columbia University, New York, comments in an editorial on the journal paper that whatever the appropriate legal intervention on drug policies turns out to be, it must be focussed on young cannabis users. The following survey substantiates that view also with respect to the link between cannabis use and crime by young people.

Lifestyle?

The Youth Lifestyle Survey carried out in 1999 by the Home Office suggests that cannabis use is one activity of a wider personal context, of which the propensity for committing crime is a strong factor.

The survey asks 3,900 young people about drug use and offending. While it found that cannabis use usually predates use of other drugs, for example, ecstasy, crime usually predates drug taking. Thus it may be concluded that drug use is a consequence of lifestyle of which cannabis, because it is more available, tends to be the first drug young people encounter.

Sources

British Lung Foundation Study (2002) *A Smoking Gun?* British Lung Foundation.
Home Office (1999) *Youth Lifestyle Survey*. Home Office.

Lynskey, M. et al. (2003) *Journal of the American Medical Association.* 289: 427–82.

Pudney, S. (2002) *The Road to Ruin?* Home Office.

The Amphetamines

Around a quarter of young people between the ages of twelve and sixteen are reported to have tried amphetamines at least once. Amphetamines are central nervous system (CNS) stimulants. The immediate effect of taking amphetamines is an increase in alertness and a decrease in feelings of fatigue and boredom. Previously difficult tasks may appear easy and the user is filled with self-confidence. Additionally, users may experience confusion and flight of ideas similar to that experienced by sufferers of manic depression during the manic phase of their illness ('flight of ideas' are lots of unconnected different thoughts whizzing around at the same time: 'Nice day out today, been to the Eiffel Tower recently? What do you think of the Russian president? That was a really good football game last week, I like cheese don't you?' This would all be said in the space of about five seconds). Auditory and tactile hallucinations may occur, sometimes of an extremely unpleasant type.

Acute and chronic symptoms of amphetamine use include rapid heartbeat, elevated blood pressure, nausea and vomiting, weight loss, agitation, chest pain, respiratory depression, and confusion. An interesting phenomena often associated with long term amphetamine use is a paranoid state closely resembling paranoid schizophrenia. Signs of amphetamine addiction or dependence often include extreme weight loss, malnutrition and impaired personal hygiene as well as the paranoia just mentioned.

Low doses were used during World War Two to keep combatants awake although care had to be taken due to rebound fatigue when the effects of the drug wore off. Additionally, they were, for a short time, prescribed for obesity as amphetamines are powerful appetite suppressants. Currently amphetamines are occasionally prescribed for narcolepsy and attention-deficit disorder (ADHD) in children. Interestingly for the adolescents suffering from ADHD, taking amphetamines has the opposite effect to that normally associated with this group of substances – it slows them down.

In their naturally occurring forms amphetamines have been used for many thousands of years. In modern times, they were discovered by an American-Chinese pharmacist named Chen who was searching for a cure for asthma. Chen came across a desert shrub that had been used for many centuries as an effective general remedy and managed to distil the alkaloid ephedrine from it. He found that ephedrine proved effective against asthma, and in searching for a synthetic substitute discovered the amphetamine group of drugs at around the time of the First World War. The drug comes in various forms, usually as tablets, but it is also possible to obtain a powder form that can be injected, snorted or smoked in the same way as heroin.

Tolerance to amphetamines develops quickly with the result that the user soon has to take handfuls of pills to maintain the effect. Alternatively, many users turn to amphetamine sulphate powder which is usually snorted, 'bombed' or injected.

Cocaine

Cocaine is a naturally occurring substance produced by the coca plant, *Erythroxylon Coca*, and like many of the drugs discussed, has been used by the population where it grows (in this case, South America) for many years. Specifically with cocaine, the leaves of the coca plant are chewed directly from the bush without preparation of any kind. It is believed that the effect of the cocaine within the leaves is mild in this form, and is used by native Indians to ward off the effects of high altitude and extreme cold.

Like the amphetamines, cocaine is a central nervous system stimulator. It has three principal actions:

1. It is a potent local anaesthetic agent and, like all other local anaesthetics, works by preventing the passage of nerve impulses down the nerve cell by blocking sodium channels that are located in the nerve membranes.
2. It is a powerful vascoconstrictor; in other words, it constricts the blood vessels.
3. It increases levels of dopamine and another chemical messenger, noradrenalin in the blood.

Cocaine has a rapid absorption rate if placed on the mucus membranes, and peak blood levels will be achieved within 30–60 minutes. Decline takes over about six hours which is one of the reasons why it primarily tends to be taken nasally.

In the peripheral nervous system (PNS) cocaine increases the flight/fight syndrome and increases heart rate and blood pressure. Additionally, it produces bronchodilation in the lungs and increases body temperature, dilates the pupils, and shifts blood flow from the stomach and intestines to the muscles. This intensity can produce hypoxia (reduction of the blood/oxygen supply) of the nasal septum which eventually results in the tissues of the nose dying. In the central nervous system (CNS), cocaine acts as a stimulant and euphoriant which affects the cortex and brain stem. It increases mental awareness and alertness and lessens weariness. Co-ordination decreases with higher doses because of the drug effects on the co-ordination centres in the brain stem.

An overdose of cocaine can cause acute depression, impatience, anxiety, sleepinesss and craving. Deaths that occur are usually due to respiratory failure, cerebral vascular accident (stroke) or cardiac arrest.

Cocaine used to be viewed as only causing psychological addiction, however recently it has been found that chronic use of cocaine leads to neurophysiological adaptation. The changes it may produce include physiological addiction. Intermittent craving for cocaine can occur months or even years after the person has stopped using the drug.

A further danger of cocaine is that it has the ability to cross the placental barrier, so intoxicating any foetus present in the user. Women who use cocaine during pregnancy are much more likely to have spontaneous abortions, placental detachment, premature labour and so forth. These effects are presumed to stem from the foetus suffering from a lack of oxygen. Some babies are also born with subtle neurological defects and nearly all babies who are born to addicted mothers are irritable, tremulous and difficult to soothe. These affected babies are just beginning to come through the schools system and reports are that they are aggressive, withdrawn, have difficulty forming attachments and have problems dealing with multiple stimuli. These children have been described as the 'bio-underclass'.

Now of course there is crack cocaine which is basically the same drug, but in a slightly different form. Crack comes as small crystals or 'rocks' which are typically smoked. The sensation caused by crack has a very rapid onset and is very intense, but only lasts for a very short while.

The Opiates

The opiates or opioids have been known to humans for centuries. The naturally occurring members of this class of drug (morphine and codeine) come from the poppy plant *Papaver Somniferum* which is found in many areas of Southern Asia and also in Turkey, Iran and various other parts of the Middle East. The opiates are found in gummy substances extracted from the seed of the poppy. Opium is produced from this substance and codeine and morphine are derived from opium. Other drugs, such as heroin, are processed from morphine or codeine.

Opiates have been used both medically and non-medically for centuries. As noted earlier, a tincture of opium called laudanum has been widely used since the 16th century as a remedy for 'nerves' or to stop coughing and diarrhoea. By the early 19th century, morphine had been extracted in a pure form suitable for solution. With the introduction of the hypodermic needle in the mid-19th century, injection of the solution became the common method of administration.

Heroin (diacetylmorphine) was introduced in 1898 and was heralded as a remedy for morphine addiction. Although heroin proved to be a more potent painkiller (analgesic) and cough suppressant than morphine, it was also more likely to produce dependence.

Of the 20 alkaloids contained in opium, only codeine and morphine are still in widespread clinical use today. In this century, many synthetic drugs have been developed with essentially the same effects as the natural opium alkaloids. Opiate-related synthetic drugs, such as methadone, were first developed to provide an analgesic that would not produce drug dependence. Unfortunately, all opiates (including naturally occurring opiate derivatives and synthetic opiate-related drugs), while effective as analgesics, can also produce dependence.

Opium appears either as dark brown chunks or in powder form, and is generally eaten or smoked. Heroin usually appears as a white or brownish powder, which is dissolved in water for injection. Most street preparations of heroin contain only a small percentage of the drug (typically only 40 per cent), as they are diluted with sugar, quinine, or other drugs and substances. Other opiate analgesics appear in a variety of forms, such as capsules, tablets, syrups, elixirs, solutions, and suppositories. Street users usually inject opiate solutions under the skin ('skin popping') or directly into a vein or muscle, but the drugs may also be 'snorted' into the nose or taken orally, rectally or, more commonly these days, smoked in tin-foil (chasing the dragon).

Effects

Short term effects appear soon after a single dose and disappear in a few hours or days. Opioids briefly stimulate the higher centres of the brain but then depress activity of the central nervous system. Immediately after injection of an opioid into a vein, the user feels a surge of pleasure or a 'rush'. This gives way to a state of gratification; hunger, pain, and sexual urges rarely intrude. The dose required to produce this effect may at first cause restlessness, nausea, and vomiting. With moderately high doses, however, the body feels warm, the extremities heavy, and the mouth dry. Soon, the user goes 'on the nod', an alternately wakeful and drowsy state during which the world is forgotten.

As the dose is increased, breathing becomes gradually slower. With very large doses, the user cannot be roused; the pupils contract to pinpoints; the skin is cold, moist, and bluish; and profound respiratory depression resulting in death may occur.

Overdose is a particular risk on the street, where the amount of drug contained in a 'hit' cannot be accurately gauged. In treatment setting, the effects of a usual dose of morphine last for three to four hours. Although pain may still be felt, the reaction to it is reduced, and the patient feels content because of the emotional detachment induced by the drug.

Drug users who share needles are also at a high risk of acquiring HIV (human immunodeficiency virus), AIDS (acquired immune deficiency syndrome) and HCV (hepatitis C virus). HIV infection eventually leads to AIDS. Unsterile injection techniques can also cause abscesses, cellulitis, liver disease, and even brain damage. Among users with a long history of injecting, tetanus is common. Pulmonary complications, including various types of pneumonia, may also result from the unhealthy lifestyle of the user, as well as from the depressant effect of opiates on respiration.

Tolerance and dependence

With regular use, tolerance develops to many of the desired effects of the opioids. As we have seen, this means the user must use more of the drug to achieve the same intensity of effect. Chronic users may also become psychologically and physically dependent on opioids. Psychological dependence exists when a drug is so central to a person's thoughts, emotions, and activities that the need to continue its use becomes a craving or compulsion. With physical dependence, the body has adapted to the presence of the drug, and withdrawal symptoms occur if use of the drug is reduced or stopped abruptly. Some users take heroin on an occasional basis, thus avoiding physical dependence.

Withdrawal from opioids, which in regular users may occur as early as a few hours after the last administration, produces uneasiness, yawning, tears, diarrhoea, abdominal cramps, goose bumps, and runny nose. These symptoms are accompanied by a craving for the drug. Major withdrawal symptoms peak between 48 and 72 hours after the last dose and subside after a week. Some bodily functions, however, do not return to normal levels for as long as six months. Sudden withdrawal by heavily dependent users who are in poor health has occasionally been fatal. Opioid withdrawal, however, is much less dangerous to life than alcohol and barbiturate withdrawal.

Opiate use in pregnancy

Opioid-dependant women are likely to experience complications during pregnancy and childbirth. Among their most common medical problems are anaemia, cardiac disease, diabetes, pneumonia and hepatitis. They also have an abnormally high rate of spontaneous abortion, breech delivery, caesarian section, and premature birth. Opioid withdrawal has also been linked to a high incidence of stillbirths.

Infants born to heroin-dependent mothers are smaller than average and frequently show evidence of acute infection. Most exhibit withdrawal symptoms of varying degrees and duration. The mortality rate among these infants is higher than normal.

Who uses opiates?

Opiates and their synthetic counterparts are used in modern medicine to relieve acute pain suffered as a result of disease, surgery, or injury; in the treatment of some forms of acute heart failure; and in the control of moderate to severe coughs or diarrhoea. They are not the desired treatment for the relief of chronic pain, because their long term and repeated use can result in drug dependence and side effects. They are, however, of particular value in control of pain in the later stages of terminal illness, where the possibility of dependence is not a significant issue.

A small proportion of people for whom opioids have been medically prescribed become dependent; they are referred to as 'medical addicts'. Even the use of non-prescription codeine products, if continued inappropriately, may get out of control. Medical advice should be sought, since withdrawal symptoms may result from abrupt cessation of use after physical dependence has been established. Because members of the medical and allied health professions have ready access to opioids, some become dependent.

As we will see in Chapter 5, although heroin is often discussed in the media, its use is still relatively rare in the UK.

The Hallucinogens (LSD and Ecstasy)

The hallucinogens (LSD and so on) are the most extraordinary of all drugs, because they have a more extreme effect than any other drug known. They come from both nature and the laboratory with many being structurally similar to various neurotransmitters found in the brain. They have been classified according to either the neurotransmitters they most closely resemble or the place in the brain they are thought to act upon.

There are many examples of this class of drug and, where understood, their actions are complex, but essentially most have the following effects: they may depress salivation, reduce sweating, increase body temperature, dilate the pupils, blur vision and increase heart rate. They also prevent secretion of stomach acid and were once used to treat duodenal ulcers. They may produce mild euphoria, profound amnesia, fatigue, delirium, drowsiness, confusion and loss of attention. Large doses can produce a state resembling a psychosis.

The most well known of this group of drugs is LSD or Lysergic Acid Diethylamide. It was first discovered by Albert Hoffman in 1938 while he was looking into possible therapeutic uses for ergot and its derivatives. LSD and the associated drugs are structurally similar to the chemical messenger serotonin. It is believed that LSD principally acts on the area of the brain which acts as a 'sorting centre' filtering out many sensations that are of only slight importance. It seems that LSD disrupts this area and so allows a surge of activity where the common becomes novel and the user is exposed to many things usually not noted on a conscious level.

When taken orally, LSD is absorbed rapidly and a dose of 25 micrograms (or one-millionth of an ounce) is usually enough to produce characteristic hallucinations. The effects of the drug are generally noticed after about 30–60 minutes and the effects can last up to 12 hours.

Physiological effects include dilation of the pupils, increased heart rate and blood pressure and increased levels of blood glucose. Psychological effects are, to say the least, unpredictable and can be affected by the mood of the user and the expectation they have about the drug.

Tolerance to LSD rapidly occurs, but physical dependence does not. Flashbacks which, at the moment, have no known causes, can occur weeks, or even years after a trip and can be brought on or made worse by marihuana use or anxiety.

Mescaline is the active ingredient of the peyote mushroom, which has been used in Mexico during religious ceremonies for centuries. When swallowed Mescaline takes about an hour to have a marked effect. At low doses it causes effects similar to peripheral nervous system arousal, but at higher doses it can cause anxiety, tremors and visual hallucinations, particularly bright coloured lights, geometric designs, animals and people. However, insight is normally maintained so that 'bad trips' tend to be rare.

Within this group of drugs is a sub-group known as the hallucinogenic amphetamines. There are over a thousand different compounds within this particular group of drugs, the best known of which being methyl-enedioxymethamphetamine (MDMA) or Ecstasy. As the term suggests, hallucinogenic amphetamines produce a combination of amphetamine like stimulation and mild sensory distortion, but their main, socially sought after effect, appears to be one of generating feelings of empathy and goodwill to all.

Methylenedioxyamphetamine (MDA) was the first of these compounds to be widely used. It was first synthesised in 1910, but it wasn't until 1939 when it underwent animal testing and then went on to be prescribed, unsuccess-fully, for Parkinson's Disease. MDMA quickly followed MDA and was available perfectly legally until the mid-1980s when it was banned from street use both in the UK and in America. This ban led to a flurry of activity when many hundreds of minutely different legal drugs were synthesised for street use. These drugs all had very similar effects, but were structurally different and therefore legal until they too, along with all other amphetamine like compounds were banned. However, in spite of this, it has recently become an extremely popular drug and although no official figures are available for current usage, it is known to be very high.

Due to the legal status of these compounds, very little is known about their mode of action. However, animal studies indicate that their basic function is to induce a massive release of the chemical messenger, serotonin. Serotonin is one of the neurotransmitters important in regulating mood, sleep, aggression and sexual activity and it is the effect that this initial flood has on these emotions that is thought to be some of the main reasons why people take Ecstasy.

A lack of research in humans has made it difficult to predict exactly what the effects of prolonged usage of MDMA might be, but animal studies indicate that Ecstasy is toxic and can produce permanent degeneration of parts of the neurons within the brain.

What is known about Ecstasy and related compounds is that they cause stimulation of the peripheral nervous system causing heart rate to accelerate, blood pressure to increase and function to be diverted away from mainten-ance systems of the body. It is these effects, coupled with the social setting in which they are generally used, which can lead to the medical problems we have all read about. However, these incidents are extremely rare.

Phencyclidine, also known as PCP or Angel Dust, is another well known, or rather infamous, drug. It was developed in 1956 as an analgesic and amnesiac agent. It was used briefly in humans as an anaesthetic, but produced bizarre reactions including agitation, disorientation, delirium and hallucinations.

Subsequently it was dropped as a human drug and is now used as an animal tranquiliser. More than any other drug, including LSD, it produces psychic disturbances that closely resemble schizophrenia. This suggests that there may be a possible relation between the effects of Angel Dust and the biochemistry of schizophrenia, however, this has yet to be substantiated.

Angel Dust is well absorbed and can be taken orally or smoked. It can produce an unresponsive state with intense analgesia and amnesia. Street doses of up to one gram can produce a prolonged coma of some days followed by a recovery period of up to two weeks which can be marked by gross confusion with various types of delusions. Other effects of taking Angel Dust include a tendency towards violence, and extremely high tolerance to pain and self-injury.

What cannot be emphasised enough is that this group of drugs is probably the most powerful and potentially devastating of all the drugs of abuse.

Certainly it is possible to overdose fatally with heroin the first time it is used, but using a typical amount of LSD in a single dose can cause irreparable psychological damage very quickly. The drugs which make up this group are not particularly physically dangerous, but the psychological damage they can cause can be immense. One of their main dangers is their unpredictability; a person may experience six hours of unbelievable bliss and happiness the first time they take one of these drugs, only to live through an equivalent period of hell the next time. Very bad experiences are relatively rare, but they do exist and taking any of these drugs is a lottery. Once a person is experiencing a bad trip there is very little they can do until the effects of the drug have run their course. As someone said 'once you're on the plane you can't get off until it lands.'

Inhalants

Almost all commonly abused inhalants are volatile hydrocarbon solvents produced from petroleum and natural gas. The term 'volatile' means that they evaporate when exposed to air. Solvent refers to their capacity to dissolve many other substances. These substances are widely used in industry as cleaning fluids, car fuel, adhesives and so on. In addition some have been designed to act as propellants in aerosols.

Generally speaking, inhalants produce a number of close related CNS depressant effects similar in nature to alcohol, sedatives and hypnotics. Small doses may produce acute symptoms which include alcohol-like intoxication as well as sensory and perceptual distortions often accompanied by delusions of grandeur. Additionally, sensations of weightlessness and dissociation from the environment may occur as well as mild feelings of euphoria. Also reported are instances of giddiness, gregariousness, emotional disinhibition, inability to co-ordinate movements and muscle weakness as well as slowed reflexes, slurred speech, impaired judgement, sensitivity to light and ringing in the ears. Hallucinations also sometimes occur as do violent outbursts against themselves and others. At high levels these drugs produce anaesthesia and sleep. Tolerance rapidly develops and psychological dependence appears to exist although it is uncertain if physical dependence occurs.

What is clear is that the use of this class of drug is extremely dangerous, often leading to death. One reason why these drugs appear to be so lethal is because they tend to be abused by very young adolescents with deaths often occurring amongst 10 and 11-year-olds. These deaths are usually the result of a heart attack or suffocation which is often caused by a person becoming unconscious whilst still having the plastic bag containing the substance over their head. In addition to death, there are other severe effects associated with chronic inhalant use including liver failure, kidney failure and occasionally brain damage.

The Benzodiazepines (Valium etc.)

This group of drugs is one of those that has caused devastating long term problems amongst a group of people who would not normally be associated with drugs of addiction, but before we discuss that aspect of them, it is interesting to delve into their history. However, it should be noted that we intend to cover this group of drugs in some depth because of their continuing importance in our society. Many millions remain addicted to them and as such they are worth serious consideration.

During the 1950s the Swiss pharmaceutical company Hoffman la Roche developed Chlordiazepoxide, a drug which they marketed under the trade name of 'Librium'. This product was the first of a long line of so called 'minor tranquilisers' which make up the Benzodiazepine (BDZ) group of drugs.

BDZs were developed in a deliberate attempt to synthesise a tranquiliser without the sedative properties of their predecessors, the barbiturates. It was also hoped that the potential for abuse, addiction and tolerance of the barbiturates would be avoided by this new group of drugs. Initially benzodiazepines were regarded as a wonder drug by health professionals and lay persons alike. They were much touted as the 'housewife's friend' and replaced gin as the traditional 'mother's little helper'. They were thought of as being a simple safe, non-addictive, cure all, for a variety of so called 'nervous disorders'. In point of fact they were none of those things although they were less acutely dangerous than their predecessors the barbiturates.

During the late 1960s and early to mid 1970s they were widely prescribed, mainly to women, for a variety of disorders from depression and anxiety to sexual dysfunctions and insomnia. It was during the mid 1970s that BDZ prescribing rose to a peak and in 1975 Diazepam (Valium) was the single most commonly prescribed drug of any kind in America, even more so than antibiotics and pain relief preparations. It was only towards the end of the 1970s that doctors and other health professionals as well as sections of the media began to realise that a culture of massive over prescribing and addiction had grown up with the use of BDZs and research has shown that abuse, addiction, tolerance and dependence develop commonly with BDZ use.

Benzodiazepines are completely absorbed when taken orally with peak plasma concentrations occurring about an hour after ingestion. Due to the fact that some of them, particularly Diazepam, can be reabsorbed from bile, a few have very long half-lives. Basically what this means is that their effects can last for a very long time indeed. Additionally, some of them can still be detected in the body of an elderly person up to two months after ingestion.

Initially the benzodiazepines were marketed for the general symptomatic treatment of anxiety and insomnia. Later this usage was extended to treat all manner of disorders including manic conditions, schizophrenia, delirium tremens and acute restlessness. For insomniacs, BDZs with long half lives used to be prescribed, so that patients woke up with a hangover effect similar to the one produced by barbiturates and remained sedated throughout the day. Nowadays, Euhypnos (Temazepam) a benzodiazepine with a half life of only three hours, is used, but Temazepam has many problems of its own and will be discussed a little later.

It is now known that even if conservative therapeutic doses are used, tolerance to benzodiazepines may develop after only a few weeks of therapy. Many recent studies have clearly documented the development of tolerance, dependence and addiction to BDZs, but there is still confusion amongst practitioners over the prescription of them. Indeed, the definition of insomnia and the need for pharmaceutical intervention at all in minor sleep disorders and non-pathological anxiety states has been brought into question.

If benzodiazepines became the drugs of choice for insomniacs they were, and still are, extensively used as tranquilisers in a variety of anxiety type disorders. In those early days of the 1960s and 1970s anxiety seemed to be defined as almost any disturbance of mood from slight agitation to depression and mania. They can certainly be of value in acute situations and, if prescribed appropriately, can be a useful tool in the management of minor neurotic disorder, however, they should be discontinued as soon as the acute episode has passed and should never be prescribed in the long term.

It is possible to cure a person's physical addiction to heroin in five days by reducing the amount taken by 20 per cent a day, but it can take 18 months to wean a person off Valium. We will now look at this process of withdrawal in some depth as it gives a good insight into the seriousness of this group of substances. Although benzodiazepines are relatively safe, (it's actually very difficult to kill yourself with a benzodiazepine overdose) in acute form at its most severe, withdrawal from Valium and other benzodiazepines can cause a patient to have an epileptic fit and, if untreated, die. They may also commit suicide. At the very least abrupt withdrawal from the drug can lead to nausea, palpitations, acute anxiety, sleeplessness, irritability, headaches, sweating and paranoia.

The following conditions were often experienced by patients following withdrawal:

- **Perceptual distortions, hallucinations and delusions**: Many patients complain of some form of perceptual distortion. Patients commonly see disembodied heads, hear bangs and thumps or tunes and are aware of misinterpreting things perceived by their senses. A common example of this would be a woman who saw a coat hanging on the back of her wardrobe and mistook it for a person. Additionally, people often feel their body is distorted or undergoing unnatural changes.
- **Paranoid thoughts and feelings of persecution**: Although most of these symptoms disappear after four weeks of abstinence, during that early time of withdrawal about 50 per cent of people report strong ideas that they are being watched and that other people are plotting ways to cause discomfort to them.
- **Memory and concentration**: Nearly all patients report experiencing a marked decrease in memory skills during their time taking benzodiazepines and this becomes worse during the withdrawal period. Concentration is also adversely affected although this becomes better after withdrawal.
- **Depersonalisation**: Over three quarters of patients say they suffer disturbing feelings of unreality or depersonalisation when withdrawing from benzodiazepines. This depersonalisation sensation often makes a person feel they are going mad and during the withdrawal process often say they experience 'windows' of time when they can see their true selves looking back out at them. As withdrawal time increases, so these windows

become longer, however, even months after withdrawal, patients say that normality can suddenly be taken away to be replaced by 'flashbacks' of depersonalisation.

- **Agoraphobia**: 95 per cent of withdrawing patients develop some degree of agoraphobia whilst taking benzodiazepines. This condition tends to get considerably worse immediately following withdrawal.
- **Mood swings**: During withdrawal many describe increasing levels of depression which comes in waves, either several times a day for short periods or for longer periods that can last for days at a time. Alternatively, periods of highs and feelings of exhilaration can also be found in most patients coming off benzodiazepines. A feeling of emotional anaesthesia, an inability to either feel happiness or sadness, has also been commonly described three to four weeks after withdrawing.
- **Craving**: All withdrawing patients report degrees of craving and, in the case of patients undergoing staged withdrawal an intense feeling of looking forward to their next dose.
- **Paresthesiae**: Withdrawing patients describe feelings of 'pins and needles', numbness or altered sensation at some time during their withdrawal. These commonly occur in the limbs, but are also reported to be present around the jaw line and tongue. The sensations have been likened to those experienced by multiple sclerosis sufferers.
- **Pain**: Severe pain is a very common symptom during the withdrawal period. Many patients complain of it to some degree with headaches and toothaches being the commonest problems. Additionally, strong pain in the extremities occurs and patients also complain of foul or metallic tastes in their mouths, often accompanied by sudden jerks of their legs and backs.
- **Ataxia**: Difficulty in walking is common and seems to be caused by a combination of sensory disturbance, muscle weakness, pain and stiffness.
- **Sensory disturbances**: Blurring of vision and double vision is also common in withdrawing patients, as is hyper sensitivity to noise, taste and smell.
- **Gastrointestinal symptoms**: Difficulty with swallowing, nausea and vomiting, abdominal pain, diarrhoea and constipation is also a known result of withdrawal from Benzodiazepines.
- **Influenza like symptoms**: Specific flu type symptoms associated with withdrawal from benzodiazepine include, weakness, dizziness, aches and pains in muscles and joints, stuffy nose and sinus pain, but interestingly, no temperature
- **Metabolic and endocrine symptoms**: Loss of appetite and weight are also common, but so is increased thirst with occasional urinary incontinence.

Three reasons have been suggested for this severe and prolonged withdrawal syndrome:

1. The drugs continue to exert a pharmacological effect long after they are undetectable in the body.
2. Benzodiazepines may induce long-lasting changes in the density or sensitivity of one or multiple neurotransmitter receptors in the brain or periphery.
3. They may cause neurological damage.

Unfortunately this severe withdrawal syndrome is very difficult to treat. Patients who have been used to taking benzodiazepines over long periods of time appear to be reluctant to seek the help of a psychiatrist. At least in the first instance, withdrawal is often undertaken as a physical therapy with only peripheral psychological support. However, in recent years there has been increasing interest in more psychologically oriented treatments with anxiety management and relaxation techniques being taught alongside the physical withdrawal programmes.

As stated earlier, there are still a large number of people in this country who are dependent on Benzodiazepines to help them through their daily lives. This is a problem that has been with us for years now and is one which we have only recognised relatively recently. In addition, over the past few years another aspect of benzodiazepine abuse has developed and that is the abuse of Temazepam, the relatively short acting benzodiazepine used for night time sedation.

Until very recently Temazepam was produced as a jelly like capsule, but the liquid core was being used by opiate addicts and others as injectable material. Manufacture of Temazepam in this form has stopped in the UK. It is now produced as a conventional tablet, but its abuse persists and is in fact growing in various parts of the country. Temazepam is not a drug which can be produced by backstreet chemists so all the supplies are coming from doctors' prescriptions; a worrying thought indeed.

Conclusions

It is hoped that this fairly in-depth look at the major drugs of abuse has helped the reader to understand some of the problems associated with their use. We will now look at some of the reasons why people take drugs.

Chapter 4

Why Do We Take Drugs?

The crucial question at the centre of this book is why do people abuse drugs and alcohol? Indeed, why do they use these substances at all? If we could answer these questions then we could probably eradicate most of the problems of substance abuse that are plaguing us today – unfortunately we can't. However, we can make some intelligent guesses.

Individual Differences

Many psychologists, TV pundits, people in the pub and probably game show hosts will offer reasons as to why having chicken vindaloo followed by ten pints of beer, a glass in the face, a night in hospital and a court appearance is a good thing to do, but at the end of the day, no-one is really too sure! A lot of people seem to enjoy doing this type of thing on a fairly regular basis in the same way as others enjoy sitting in a smoke filled room and deciding after several hours of lacklustre debate to visit the local garage for some more cigarette papers!

Exactly why individuals do these things, and in fact why they choose a glass of beer over a spliff, is open to debate, but it may well have some connection with why some people hurl themselves down mountains on skis or out of perfectly functional aircraft dangling beneath flimsy canopies. The reasons may also be connected to why a happily married man with a good job, possibly an MP, of excellent standing in the community and a pillar of the local church would wager everything he has worked hard for since he was a child for ten (more likely five) minutes of unprotected sex with a teenage prostitute. Thought about in the cold light of day, it doesn't really add up at all.

These types of activities along with many others simply seem to form a part of the human condition, particularly when we are younger, and have been described by psychologist Marvin Zuckerman as 'sensation seeking' or 'risk taking' behaviours. He sees people who do these activities as being high in the personality trait of sensation seeking which he also describes as a biological or rather physiological function in which levels of the neurotransmitter dopamine are measurably different in high sensation seeking people. His theories are still under discussion, but they do seem to have some sound basis in fact and the reason for mentioning them at this point is to introduce the concept of individual difference.

The trait of sensation seeking is a relative concept and can be used to good effect to illustrate these differences using somewhat extreme examples.

Anyone reading this book in the UK will be familiar with a group of people called train spotters. These are people who do just that, they spot trains and, as far as we know they are a uniquely British phenomenon. If you travel on the British train network, sooner rather than later you will see huddled in thick quilted coats and knitted hats the 'trainspotter'. At the end of virtually every main line station small groups of these almost exclusively male white Anglo Saxon trainspotters lurk. Individuals always carry a packet of sandwiches, notebooks and pencils and write down the registration numbers of trains as they go past. Quite why they record these numbers is unknown, but they've been doing it since the days of steam, a subject best avoided if talking to them. In one of his Hitchhiker books Douglas Adams said that the second most mind bogglingly boring activity in the known universe was Vogon poetry. Clearly to most of us the most boring is writing down train numbers, but to some this activity appears to be almost orgasmic in nature.

Why?

As already mentioned, sensation seeking is a relative concept. Some trainspotters may consider standing at the end of one of the main London stations the height of excitement while others may soon tire of this activity and swiftly progress to the ultimate trainspotting activity, the ill documented 'night spot'. Although this may sound flippant, there is a serious point to be made. Some people may become extremely excited by watching the 0227 from Manchester to London meander past and find themselves going weak at the knees whilst another person from a similar cultural and socio-economic background may need to dangle off Everest or bungie jump from the Eiffel Tower to achieve the same sensation.

Why?

Unfortunately, once again, we simply don't know the answer. What we do know is that this brief discussion serves to illustrate the point of individual differences or rather, to use a very politically incorrect phrase, to show that what is one man's meat is another man's potatoes. It is with this essential point in mind that we can move into our discussion of theories of why people abuse drugs and alcohol.

Theories of Substance Abuse

There are far too many theories that attempt to explain the reason behind humans' continuing desire to alter their state of consciousness.

As we discussed at the beginning of this book the BioPsychoSocial (BPS) collection of theories are currently in vogue and, intuitively, seem to be the ones closest to the mark. However, before discussing that approach it seems necessary to review some of the more important and influential earlier theories so that it can become apparent why this book has adopted a BPS attitude. In fact the BPS approach is made up of a collection of other theories, so it is important to understand some of these.

It should however be pointed out that many people still subscribe to these individual theories and there is still merit in some of these older ideas. It should also be noted that the theories about to be discussed are by no means an exhaustive list of those available. At the last count there were a couple of hundred, but the ones that follow represent some of the more mainstream areas under consideration.

In reviewing these various models, no attempt has been made to study them in great depth. However, what has been attempted is to give a clear understanding about some of the main tenets of each different type of model and why, on the whole, they have not succeeded in satisfactorily explaining substance abuse.

Broadly speaking, most theories of addiction fall into one or more of four major categories:

- Disease model
- Biological model
- Psychological model
- Lifestyle model

The Disease Model

The Disease Model provides a major part of the justification for excessive, ineffective drug control policies and supports values that are repellent outside the drug field.

(Alexander, 1987).

The modern concept of addiction as a disease is based on theories advanced by Jellinek (1960) when discussing alcoholism and is the casual model adopted by all the self-help groups such as Alcoholics Anonymous (AA), Narcotics Anonymous (NA) and Gamblers Anonymous (GA). The Disease

Figure 4.1 Disease Models of Addiction (Alexander, 1987)

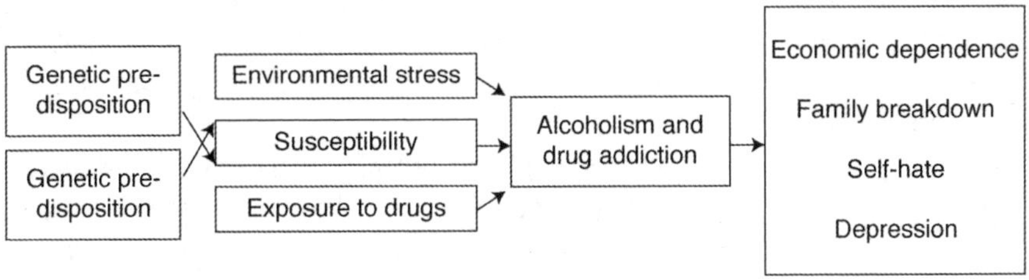

concept has been around considerably longer than the last few decades and first became widely acknowledged during the late 1930s with the formation of AA. As we will see later, the Disease Model is sometimes known as the 'Cop Out Model' as it allows people to say things along the lines of 'I can't help being an (insert the addiction of your choice). I'm suffering from an illness'. This follows along similar lines of a cancer sufferer saying they can't help feeling rough as they're terminally ill. Unfortunately for the various types of substance abuser, the argument doesn't quite hold water, as we will see later. Having said that, in 1956 the American Medical Association (AMA) finally accepted AA's concepts of the Disease Model when they formally classified alcoholism as a medical disease.

It should be noted that the Disease Model is not exemplified by one straight forward theory, there are literally dozens of variations ranging from Milam and Ketcham's (1983) definition which sees addiction as an incurable all-or-nothing unitary disorder caused solely by hereditary physical abnormalities to Miller's (1993) suggestions of the Disease Model as part of a more BPS construct. When discussing the Disease Model here, an attempt will be made to refer to a broad synthesis of all the popular variations of the model. However, before it is possible to discuss the merits, or otherwise, of the Disease Model as it relates to substance abuse, it is necessary to look at precisely what a 'disease' actually is.

Acker (1993) maintained that it is impossible to say whether addiction can be explained as a disease process alone because the definition of the term 'disease' is itself, extremely fluid. Certainly the perception of disease as a concept has altered over the years, often in tune with advancements in medical techniques.

In a slightly simplistic sense, it may be possible to describe disease as any condition that is diagnosable and treatable in medical terms where the cause of the condition is not under the control of the victim. However, it might be appropriate to delve a little more deeply into the concept of disease as this idea, particularly the reference to 'control' may not only be simplistic, but may also be rather too rigorous to be of practical value. After all, most conditions have an element of choice within their causes, be they coronary heart disease, cancer or, to an extent, diabetes.

Generally, it is possible to say that philosophical approaches to disease can be described as ontological or functionalist. the ontological view maintains that diseases are real, tangible, entities that do not exist in abstraction. In this way diseases that are caused by bacteria may be classified as Ontological and this view has proved useful in overcoming and eradicating certain diseases where it has been possible to describe a casual organism, chart its life course and develop agents that will act against it. However, by taking an ontological approach it is possible to dehumanise an individual and to treat only the condition they are suffering from. In addition, by taking an ontological approach and granting a disease 'independent status' there is a danger in expecting standardised treatments to work in all cases, which obviously doesn't happen. On the other hand, the functionalist approach to disease places the individual at the centre of the condition which is then treated as an imbalance and takes an altogether more holistic approach than the ontological conception of disease. The functionalist approach was common prior to the 19th century, but went out of favour after the industrial revolution as scientists began to have the ability to discover specific disease causing organisms.

Gradually ontology took over until the only conditions that practitioners sought to explain from a functionalist standpoint were the psychiatric ones, mainly because they couldn't be explained any other way. Nowadays however, medical science appears to be combining the two approaches acknowledging, for instance, that a bad dose of Asian flu may have ontological origins but the speed of a patient's recovery may have functionalist aspects too.

Generally, the question of a specific pathological condition being a disease or otherwise, does not seem important as it once did. After all, coronary heart disease is clearly classified as a disease, but, like addiction, the biological cause is somewhat vague.

On a more practical level, however, it might be appropriate to follow Talbott's (1986) suggestions that in order for a condition to be a formal disease it needs to fulfil five categories or assumptions:

- A disease should be a primary condition, not a secondary symptom.
- A disease should involve a recognisable set of signs and symptoms that permit accurate diagnosis.

- A disease should have clearly established etiological agents and causes.
- A disease should bring about specific anatomical and physiological changes in an affected individual.
- A disease should have a predictable and progressive course.

Talbott's suggestions do have intuitive merit and, at a glance, various common conditions can be seen to fulfil the paradigm's tenets. Can it be used as a model by which to classify addiction or substance abuse as a disease? We wish that it could, would that life were so simple.

Before we consider Talbott's suggestions further we need to mention a term which will crop up rather a lot from here called 'direction of causality'. Frankly this concept is a considerable nuisance when considering causes of substance abuse. Essentially it is the chicken or egg syndrome. An example: Later on it will be seen that low marks at school are associated with drug use. The question is though, did the fact that a young person was stoned cause them to do badly at school or did the fact that they were doing badly at school drive them to drugs? That is a slightly simplistic way of describing the problem or direction of causality, but it gets the point across. Direction of causality issues are major stumbling blocks in addiction research.

If we examine the first of Talbott's points, that a disease should be a primary condition, not a secondary symptom we immediately run into problems, especially if we consider this direction of causality question. Talbott supported his thesis by citing a study of 500 doctors undergoing treatment for a chemical dependency in which 94 per cent failed to present with a primary psychiatric diagnosis of sufficient severity to explain their addiction. It was noted that nearly three-quarters of the sample complained of emotional symptoms which he described as being secondary to their dependence. Champions of the Disease Model might well cite this work as evidence for their cause, but there are serious flaws within the study. As alluded to earlier, the direction of causality of the reported emotional symptoms must be called into question and the fact that 94 per cent of the sample did not present with an identifiable psychotic illness is hardly conclusive evidence that substance dependence is the primary condition. Additionally, 500 physicians cannot really be deemed a representative sample of typical substance abusers and no control subjects appear to have been used. Having said that, it is still possible that addiction is a primary disease, particularly in light of more recent work in biochemistry and genetics, so Talbott's first premise could apply and addiction could be a primary condition, not a secondary symptom.

The second of Talbott's points, that a disease involves a recognisable set of signs and symptoms that permit accurate diagnosis, would seem easy to apply to addictive disorders and non-specific substance abuse in general. Although an individual's responses to different drugs can vary, a person presenting as an addict or heavy abuser will suffer from craving, withdrawal, tolerance and so on. Talbott lists seven associated signs that he says are typical of a person in an addictive state: compulsivity; destruction of physical health; deteriorating emotional health; social/cultural/spiritual depravity; abnormal tolerance; withdrawal and blackouts or amnesia. Whilst some of these states such as withdrawal may agree with many mainstream theories, others such as 'spiritual depravity' do test the boundaries of credibility somewhat. Nevertheless this second proposition is at least reasonable and can be generally supported. One might at this point accept the premise that a broad range of symptoms need not necessarily exclude substance abuse from being classified as a disease. This position is supported if one compares an addictive state with other, recognised diseases. For example, schizophrenia, a condition clearly given disease status, often does not display indicative signs until the condition is severe and yet psychiatrists seem to have no trouble in diagnosing it, even in young people who are only displaying mild symptoms.

Proposition three that a disease has clearly established etiological agents and causes, is much harder to apply to substance abuse. The causology of substance abuse is the focus of much of this work. However for the purpose of this section it can be said that much attention has been applied to the area and, as yet, no clear etiological agents have been indisputably identified.

The penultimate of Talbott's suggestions that disease brings about specific anatomical and physiological changes in an affected individual appears one of the simplest to apply to the addictive states. It is clear that all drugs of abuse can bring about both physical and psychological changes specific to the class of substance used. For instance, chronic overuse of alcohol can cause Korsakoff's Syndrome and cirrhosis of the liver while the amphetamines can place undue strain on the cardiovascular system and give rise to a paranoid state. Additionally, prolonged opiate abuse depletes an individual's own endorphin levels and marijuana can cause respiratory problems and memory-learning problems. This particular condition, that addiction brings about anatomical and physiological changes, can also be applied to non-substance addictions such as (possibly) marathon running and gambling.

Finally, Talbott's fifth proposition is that a disease has a predictable and progressive course. If one is seeking to support the Disease Model of addiction, it may be possible to do so in this context by applying Jellinek's four phases of alcoholism. Jellinek described the four phases as:

- The pre-alcoholic symptomatic phase where alcohol (and presumably other drugs) are used to reduce levels of stress.
- The prodromal phase which is characterised by fugue states, secretiveness and denial.
- The crucial phase which is typified by a loss of control.
- The final chronic phase which is typified, in alcoholism, by reverse tolerance, loss of memory, and social, moral and ethical deterioration.

Even allowing for individual differences, if this proposition can be supported, it might be expected that Jellinek's four phases could, broadly, be followed. However, there has been a considerable amount of work published that indicates that this is not the case. For instance, Marlatt (1983) supports the position of controlled drinking, a stance that runs counter to Jellinek's ideas and the Disease Model as a whole. He maintains that total abstinence is not necessary to a full recovery and research which has recorded a spontaneous remission rate of up to 40 per cent of alcoholics also lends weight to critics of Jellinek's theory and, by implication, Talbott's fifth proposition. However, given the broad base of symptoms just mentioned, is it any wonder that substance abuse does not always follow a reliable course?

This possible lack of predictability of an addiction course is not by any means unique and need not bar it from a classification as a disease. For example, syphilis is certainly classified as a disease and yet progression to the recognised final stages only occurs in a minority of cases. There is no way to predict which third of patients will develop this terminal phase, and yet that does not stop syphilis being a disease.

Even if all Talbott's five propositions were fulfilled by substance abusers, and as has been discussed, there is much question over them being relevant to the field of addictive behaviours, this would still not be total proof that addiction and substance abuse is a disease in the same mould as cancer.

Despite the possible fluidity of the precise definition of disease, the Disease Model, particularly if one utilises a combined ontological-functionalist approach, has long been applied, in various guises, to both alcohol and drug addiction. The Disease Model treats addiction as a progressive illness which leads to personality problems affecting emotional and cognitive functioning.

However, we suggest that even if this model is useful as an overall concept, it may not be possible to apply it to everyone. Let us revert to media generated stereotypes for a moment: take for instance a white, middle class substance abuser with a family and a reasonable job who undergoes treatment. To that person addiction may well be seen as a disease, but might the same be true of the African-American whose only employment is in trafficking and who spends considerable time in prison and is never exposed to a treatment programme? In spite of this stereotypical view of people, these observations do suggest that 'disease', particularly in this context, is a relative term and can mean many different things to many diverse groups of people. Indeed, Shaffer and Robbins in 1991 went so far as to say that the question 'is addiction a disease?' can never be definitively answered because the Disease Model is purely a cultural construction.

We can support this criticism if we look at the related area of poverty. If we consider the position of a person in the Third World who has no material possessions and little food they are clearly poor by just about anyone's standard. However, if we take a person in the UK who is living close to the poverty line on state benefits, but who has just about enough food to thrive on, owns a television, video and so on are they poor? They might be able to afford cigarettes and a couple of pints of beer a week, but are they poor? Compared with the starving person in the Third World clearly not, but within the context of the society in which they live they may well be considered poor. In the same way the concept of a disease does seem to vary from society to society. To be slightly trite, the starving individual in the Third World might say they have never been given the opportunity to test the Disease Model of addiction. In a similar way people who use large amounts of cannabis as part of their religious beliefs or who smoke opium as part of a cultural tradition might, if taken out of the contexts of their society, be considered victims of the disease of addiction, but within context are perfectly normal.

The other main problem with the Disease Model is summed up by our alternative name for it: 'The Cop out Model'. The model clearly helps addicts to accept their dependency and reduce any possible shame and guilt (which must be good). It may also help the community to accept the problems associated with addiction and to take responsibility by instigating preventative programmes. It may also help abusers in treatment to completely shed any guilt feeling and therefore concentrate on their recovery without moral burdens. However, if a less liberal stance is taken, the Disease Model may also be seen as allowing abusers to abrogate all responsibility and allow them an excuse if relapse occurs. On the other hand it might be said that it allows the abuser to take the stance that they are not responsible for the disease but are fully responsible for recovery which is something of a compromise position.

However, the reverse of this particular coin is that addicts are 'powerless over their addiction' as some of the AA tracts pronounce and this could be interpreted that they are normally weak individuals who are unable to cope with the strains existing in a society or, as Lawrence Kolb in 1925 suggested, that substance abusers were, '. . . little men with powerful social ambitions, but without the requisite abilities to fulfil them . . .' Other researchers, more recently than Kolb, are in agreement and do not view the Disease Model favourably. Szasz (1974) suggests that the model erodes the human capacity for taking responsibility for one's actions and Walters (1992) notes that among the model's drawbacks is the inattention to such issues as personal responsibility, self-efficacy, and autonomy, and its resistance to empirical evaluation.

It may also be argued that the Disease Model cannot be accurate because of the natural remission in self-cures mentioned earlier. However, those who argue this point may have neglected that persons suffering from physical, or ontological illnesses, such as flu do, on occasion, become spontaneously well. Additionally, to refute this criticism of the Disease Model, it might be appropriate to add at this point that flu, left untreated, will eventually 'burn itself out', as the body becomes resistive to it. Might not the same possibility exist for the addictive conditions?

Alexander (1987) has indicated that the Disease Model may, at least in part, be politically motivated and provides a major part of the justification for drug control policies and supports values that are controversial outside the drug research field. Certainly it does not appear unreasonable to assume that this may be, at least superficially true. In support of Alexander's views one could simply look at the negative implications on direct employment that a relaxation in control policies would have.

In addition, the Disease Model has been used to justify America's ongoing 'War on Drugs' with traffickers preying on the sick and, with Holland as the notable exception, this attitude has been taken up by all European countries with punitive punishments being handed down to even petty offenders.

In conclusion, the Disease Model has a number of strengths and severe weaknesses. On the plus side is the fact that it is a simple theory to understand and opens up the addiction field to lay persons. Additionally, by removing any shame or guilt that might be present in an addict, it encourages attendance at treatment centres, particularly those following the Minnesota Model (Alcoholics Anonymous) where addicts know they will not be censured. On the down side, the model provides individuals with an excuse for their excesses and tends to cause the addict to become reliant on treatment philosophies. There is also a tendency to group sufferers together and not take into account individual differences, with addicts who question the system, being said to be in denial. Possibly the most serious criticism of the model is that, very much like the Freudian theory, it has many intuitively good points, but is almost impossible to evaluate from within a scientific framework.

The Disease Model, like many other models in this area, has gone in and out of favour with researchers over the years. Currently, it appears reasonable to say that the Disease Model is not capable, on its own, of explaining causes of addiction, but may well be useful in combination with other theories of offering at least a partial explanation.

The Adaptive Model

The Adaptive Model of addiction is a contemporary of the Disease Model, but may be considered a more humane and, so it is argued, a more effective model.

As can be seen from the diagram below, at the heart of the Adaptive Model is a combination and interaction of faulty upbringing, environmental inadequacy and genetic unfitness. It is considered that these factors may be primarily responsible for setting the individual on the path to the next stage of addiction which, Alexander suggests, is a general failure to develop into a mature adult. It is this failure to mature that leads to '*social ostracism, despair, mental disintegration and ultimately suicide*' (Alexander, 1987: 49) and causes the individual urgently to seek out alternative ways of achieving integration with a peer group. It is this way of reacting to an inadequate personality and maturity status that causes the susceptible individual to invoke adaptation to alcohol and drugs as a form of defence mechanism.

Figure 4.2 The Adaptive Model of Addiction (Alexander, 1987)

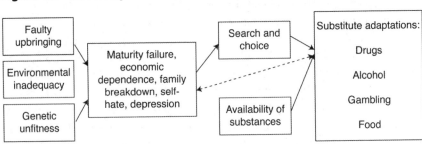

Unlike the Disease Model, the Adaptive Model does not assume that a pathology is at the base of an addiction, instead the model suggests that people are responding and adapting, within the restrictive limits of their own abilities, to their negative situation. Also in contrast to the Disease Model which sees addiction as causing numerous, often insurmountable problems, the Adaptive Model sees addiction as a result of these problems.

One of the crucial differences between the Disease Model and the Adaptive Model is that whilst the former states that addicts are powerless over their addiction the latter sees addicts as masters over their own destiny with responsibility for their decisions and actions. In addition, the Adaptive Model does not assume that the substance abuser is out of control as do many supporters of the Disease Model.

Is it possible to find support for the Adaptive Model of addiction? At the causal core of the Adaptive Model is an individual's failure to mature and integrate with peers. Alexander suggested that evidence supporting the notion that integration failure leads directly to addiction can be found in correlational studies that, he claims, have found that the majority of addicts have a background that includes sexual abuse, violence, emotional cruelty and an over-dependence on parents.

Unfortunately what Alexander does not say is why many of the individuals who have suffered this type of abuse do not turn to drugs as an adaptation. This is similar to the argument often used in court cases of sexual abuse. The accused is often said to have been abused themselves and the response from the jury is almost invariably along the lines of, yes, that is unfortunate but most abusees do not go on to become abusers. In the same way it may be true that 99.9 per cent of heroin addicts have smoked cannabis, but only something like 1 per cent of cannabis users go on to become heroin abusers.

Supporters of this model also argue that when a species is nearing the capacity that can be easily supported by the environment around it, many of the developing individuals within each generation fail to mature and are not integrated into the adult population. The logic of this argument is that as our planet becomes ever more overcrowded many of us will subconsciously turn to various means of self-destruction in order to free up resources for our genetically stronger counterparts. Possibly the weaker of us could all leap lemming like from the nearest cliff!

At the risk of denigrating our profession, this sounds like the sort of reasoning that gets psychology a bad name. It ranks alongside the Freudian type of idea that cigarette smokers smoke because they are a) symbolically suckling at their mothers breast or b) latent male homosexuals.

If this idea held any credence at all then it would seem logical that it would only be people from deprived inner cities who became substance abusers and, as we know, many affluent people have addiction problems. Surely humans are sentient creatures, capable of self-determination and rational decision making processes, is it reasonable therefore to compare addictive behaviour to lemming type instincts?

Finally, Alexander suggests that '. . . if addiction serves as a way of adapting to integration failure, it should cease if integration is subsequently achieved'. (Alexander, 1990: 47). Unfortunately for the model this doesn't tend to happen and anyway, is it reasonable to expect an individual to achieve successful integration if they are addicted?

The Adaptive Model is interesting and not without merit, but it suffers from one of the major faults of the Disease Model in that it is very hard to imagine how to test it. Until a way is found to quantify this model then it will remain little more than an attractive, some might say intuitively attractive, theoretical model, regrettably with little or no practical applications.

Biological Models

It may be possible to link Disease Models with Biological Models, particularly amongst lay persons as the concept of 'disease' often implies abnormal, or pathological, underlying physical process. For the sake of this work the models discussed here will be confined to those with a genetic or neurochemical basis and this section will be sub-divided into those two areas. However, before this discussion begins, it should be stated that strong evidence has come to light during the past two decades that biological traits or abnormalities do appear to be present in those persons vulnerable to substance abuse and addiction, both on the genetic and the neurochemical level. This evidence is not overwhelming and like all the other models mentioned, Biological Theories do offer hope of a causal explanation particularly, but not on their own. They are only a part of the picture, how large a part has yet to be determined.

Neurochemical theories

Neurochemical theories are the ones which basically say that there is a chemical imbalance in the control systems of the brain. Obviously there are imbalances after a person has been ingesting copious amounts of alcohol or cocaine for many years, but these theories say that this imbalance actually exists prior to the person using substance. This leads to some intriguing possibilities which will be discussed later in the book.

Unfortunately all neurochemical theories are exceedingly complex and involve a great deal of terminology which is incomprehensible to anyone but extremely specialised scientists and there doesn't seem much to be gained from going into it all here as it would only cloud the issues at hand.

Briefly, most of these theories concentrate on various different areas of the control centres of the brain and involve a chemical known as dopamine. Dopamine is an exceedingly important neurotransmitter, a lack of which is involved in Parkinson's Disease and an excess of which is implicated in the causes of schizophrenia.

There are four main reasons for supporting neurochemical theories as being causal in addiction:

- Addiction to alcohol and other drugs often occur in combination.
- There is evidence from twin and other types of genetic work that there may be a common biological vulnerability to substance abuse.
- Multiple addictions can be identified as independent disorders in alcohol and other drug users.
- Recent human and animal work has shown neurochemical, neurophysiological, neuropharmacological and psychopharmacological mechanisms common to alcohol and other specific drug addictions.

Also there are strong commonalities between the actions of very different types of substance and this data by itself leads one to suppose that neurochemical links exist. Examples of this for alcohol, cocaine and the opioids can be seen in the table below.

Over recent years a reasonable body of work has been built up that has examined the neurochemical mechanism pertaining to withdrawal and it appears that many substances commonly abused share withdrawal effects associated with an area of the brain known as the locus ceruleus. Withdrawal of substances such as alcohol, opioids and the benzodiazepines (Valium and so on) over excite this area and trigger effects described in the Table 4.1.

All substances of abuse are taken, at least in the first instance, to provide pleasure for the user and if one looks at the properties of various drugs, the hypothesis that they all provide pleasure in a similar way does not seem intuitively unreasonable. However, the question, 'so what' springs prominently to mind. Even if these drugs do all operate in a similar way it does not actually get us any closer to answering the question of why some people become users and others abusers.

Table 4.1 Neurochemical links

Drug	Effects of intoxication	Effects of withdrawal
Alcohol: Depressant.	Characteristic of a depressant: Incoordination, slurred speech, unconsciousness, unsteady gait, slow thinking, decreased self-control, impaired memory, irritability, blackouts, euphoria and depression.	Characteristic of a stimulant: Tremor, perspiration, dilated pupils, seizures, restlessness, anxiety, panic attacks, paranoid, illusions, disorientation and hallucinations.
Cocaine: Stimulant.	Characteristic of a stimulant: Dilated pupils, rapid heart-beat, elevated temperature, elevated blood pressure, flushed skin, euphoria, emotional lability, anorexia and anxiety.	Characteristic of a depressant: Depression, anxiety, sleeplessness, fatigue, suicidal ideas, apathy and bulimia.
Opioids: Depressant.	Characteristic of a depressant: Hypotension, slow heartbeat hypothermia, eyesight problems constriction.	Characteristic of a stimulant: Yawning, perspiration, diarrhoea, anxiety and agitation.

Genetic theories

Genetic theories are generally fairly user friendly and, on some levels, very understandable. 'My dad was an alcoholic, he passed on his genes to me therefore I'm probably going to be an alcoholic too'. This is nice, neat, and convenient. Unfortunately, as you may well have noted by now, things are rarely this straightforward in the area of substance abuse.

The genetic theories of addiction are linked to the Disease Model discussed earlier and many of the same arguments and criticisms apply equally to the two models. The key premise of the genetic group of theories is that there is a direct and traceable hereditary route down which addiction tendencies can be traced.

It may be more valuable however, not to attempt to look at genetics as a causal model, but, especially in the light of the BPS model, to look upon substance abusers as having a genetic *predisposition* or genetic *sensitivity*. This, in combination with other factors to be discussed later, might contribute to the existence of an addictive state. Certainly, for the past fifteen years or so, authors appear to be considering any genetic link to addiction to be, at the very least, polygenic and interacting with environmental factors.

There are numerous classic pieces of work in this area, but two in particular stand out and these will be used to illustrate some of the positive and negative aspects of the genetic theories of addiction.

The first was by Vaillant (1983). In a series of experiments he looked at the prevalence of alcoholism among men who had no alcoholic relatives. His basic findings were that in a group where the subjects had no familial contact with alcoholism, between 10 per cent and 14 per cent became dependent on alcohol at some time in their lives compared to between 29 per cent and 34 per cent of men who did have family contact with alcoholics.

Superficially, this evidence seems to be strongly supporting a genetic link in the onset of alcoholism. However there are several flaws, the most serious being the social, not genetic effect, that having familial contact with alcoholic relatives would have. It appears possible to assume that those persons who grew up in contact with alcoholic relatives did so in families where the attitudes towards alcohol were vastly different to those subjects whose lives were untouched by alcoholism. Bearing this in mind, the initial strong appearances of the genetic data must be completely confounded by the environmental factors.

Goodwin looked at the problem from the perspective of adoption studies in the mid-70s and early 80s and his strongest finding was that 15 per cent of male children of alcoholics who had been adopted by non-alcoholic parents were diagnosed as alcoholic at the time of the study, whereas only 4 per cent of adopted males whose natural parents were not alcoholics received the alcoholic diagnosis. Superficially, this seems like a very significant effect, males whose natural parents are alcoholics are at four times greater risk than subjects without that biological predisposition. However, if one looks at that figure from an alternative standpoint it begins to look less impressive. Essentially, what the data means is that 85 per cent of men with alcoholic parents do not become alcoholic.

In addition to the actual figures themselves being less than impressive, the methodology employed by Goodwin can also be called into question. He obtained data in the first instance, from Denmark, where interviews were recorded in Danish, translated into English, transcribed and sent to America where a psychiatrist made a diagnosis based solely on those transcripts. Goodwin then compared this data with the prevalence of alcohol reported in the general population by the Danish health authorities. This method of data collection is fatally flawed and renders any conclusions Goodwin drew as very questionable.

Another problem when looking at genetics to provide an answer to an individual's vulnerability to addictive conditions is that, by and large, social variables have been ignored. For example, exposure to illegal drugs is rarely considered. The Epidemiologic Catchment Area Study of 1990 estimated that in the United States of America lifetime opioid use and dependence was approximately 0.7 per cent of the population, far below what one might expect from genetic indicators unless one factor is exposure to drugs. If genetic theories of vulnerability to addiction are accepted it might be expected that a person with strong genetic links to addiction would actively seek the substance they needed, but clearly this does not happen. Who is to say whether these people would heavily abuse drugs or alcohol if they were exposed to them in a social setting?

Another methodological problem when looking at genetic data is that it is rarely 'clean'. For example, drug users do not tend to restrict their addiction to one particular substance, but instead might take a multitude of different preparations, all with differing pharmacological actions. In this way, it is impossible to study the possible genetic transmission of one particular drug.

Another layer of complexity is the fact that, particularly with illicit drugs, there often seems to be a secondary diagnosis existing within the primary framework of addiction. This may be depression or generalised anti-social personality disorder and, as can be seen later, if one attempts to take these conditions into consideration, one is faced with issues of direction of causality. This is an area that has caused personality theorists a lot of problems when considering addictive behaviours.

These factors, along with the 'cop out' criticism make genetic theories difficult to accept on their own. Having said that, there does not appear to be a genetic link and as research on the human genome mapping programme progresses it is expected that this link will come further into focus.

Psychological Models

Psychological models are the ones which deal not with the physical brain, but the mind within (or alongside, depending on your point of view). These theories basically say that it is our cognitions, our thoughts and emotions, which make us into substance abusers. There are very many psychological theories and we will look at only a couple of the more straighforward (and, let's be honest, sometimes less bizarre ones). Additionally we will look at these rather briefly, really simply saying what they are and how useful they are. The arguments and counter-arguments can be torturous and may only be of interest to academics (and academic trainspotters!).

The Tension Reduction Hypothesis

The Tension Reduction Hypothesis (TRT) was originally formulated by Conger, in 1956 and was developed along conditioning lines in which substance use is seen as constantly being rewarded. This basically follows the same lines as the theory behind a child who does well at school receiving praise and so trying harder, doing better, receiving proportionally more praise, trying harder, doing better and so on and so forth.

Conger originally conceived the TRT in particular relation to alcoholism, but it does not seem unreasonable to apply it equally to substances other than alcohol, even when the pharmacological effect of the drug being used is different to that of alcohol.

It is an attractive theory and one that has found broad support amongst the lay public because it seems intuitively accurate, but as with many theories of addiction, it does not appear to be the only answer. Certainly we may, on occasion, drink to relieve tension, but does that lead to alcoholism and what about stimulant drugs such as cocaine? Smokers may have an occasional cigarette when something irritating happens, but a one off irritation cannot account for a forty a day habit.

Cooper summed up the reservations about the model in 1992 when he said that:

. . . tension reduction theories of alcohol use are overly broad and individual characteristics must be considered to account for stress-related effects on alcohol use and abuse.

(Cooper, 1992: 139).

The Lifestyle Model

The Lifestyle Model considers that an individual's abuse of chemicals is not a primary disorder, but rather a reflection of a 'peculiar style of thinking'. Specifically, Walters, who developed the model, suggested in 1992 that drug usage may be an expression of an underlying criminality which, whilst not always expressed, is lying dormant in the person's psyche.

Essentially the Lifestyle Model is a collection of traits that Walters says makes up the 'typical' addict. He says that the Lifestyle Model is typified around several main types of deviant behaviour: irresponsibility and pseudo-responsibility, where addicts fail to meet responsibilities to employers, family and friends, but can, on occasion retain a veneer of responsibility that is more apparent than real due to a lack of depth and commitment; Stress-Coping

Imbalance, where addicts are unable to deal appropriately with stress and use drugs to relieve excessive stress levels that build up because they have not learned effective and appropriate coping strategies; Interpersonal Triviality where the user lacks meaningful personal interactions and seeks out other drug users for purely, drug based, superficial relationships and Social Rule Breaking where, Walters says, the addict is less interested in breaking rules than in circumventing them so that drug using activities can be indulged in.

Walters also suggests that addicts suffer from generalised cognitive distortions, specifically mollification where addicts and abusers blame their current drug related problem on others instead of accepting responsibility for their using behaviour; Entitlement where addicts give themselves permission to use drugs on such premises as having a bad day at work and Superoptimism which, Walters says, can almost be classed as grandiose thinking where the addicts often believe that they have their use of chemicals under control and do not believe that they are, or could become, addicted.

The Lifestyle Model also suggests that addiction has a recognisable and predictable course. The Pre-Drug Stage is described as the stage when people between the ages of about 12 and 21 experiment with drugs out of boredom, peer pressure and the search for new sensations. Walter notes that this stage is very common among young people today, but states only a small minority of people actually go on to the next stage that he terms Early Drug Stage. This stage tends to occur around the early 20s and early 30s and is a preliminary commitment to a drug orientated lifestyle. The addict, as they have now become, will become the salient driving force behind their actions. The Advanced Drug Stage occurs generally after the early 30s and it is during this phase that the user will appear most out of control. It is also during this stage that most contact will be had with the police and hospitals following overdose and, possibly, suicide attempts. It tends to be during this phase that most direct deaths from drugs occur. The final stage described by the Lifestyle Model is the Drug Burnout and Maturity Stage and tends to occur after about the age of 40. Walters is at pains to point out that entry into this stage is by no means the norm with many users electing to stay in the preceding Advance Drug Stage. However, if a person does enter this final stage it tends to be characterised by only sporadic drug use. Walters suggests that individuals may enter this stage due to changes in cognitions, values and motives or alternatively because there is a decline in the pleasure perceived by drug use.

Walters admits that there is no empirical evidence to support the Lifestyle Model, but maintains that one of its advantages over the more traditional

Disease Model is that it would not be hard to apply empirical principles to it. However, to those of us who are basically cynics at heart, this of course leads to the question of why the theory has not undergone empirical testing, if it is easy to do. A scientist who develops and promotes a new theory will always try to support it with firm evidence, so why has it not happened in this case?

Although it is, at least superficially, an attractive and relatively simple theory to understand, it is, like so many theories before it, flawed by this lack of supportive evidence.

The Addictive Personality

The role of personality in addiction has long been an area of extreme contention. Personality psychology has been an area of interest ever since psychology's formative years at the turn of the century and numerous theories of personality have been suggested since that time. In fact everyone from Freud to the local barman has their own theory of personality and each are equally hard to support. Although many of these theories are radically different from each other, some being trait theories, others taking a humanistic approach and still others approaching the problem from a social learning perspective, all of them share in common the desire to gain an insight into, and an explanation for, human behaviour. Everyone seems keen to be able to explain the key question of exactly *why* people do things.

Following a decline in the 1960s and early 1970s the field of personality research has recently been receiving a great deal of attention. From the plethora of studies and theories that have been published, Costa and McCrae's Five Factor Theory of Personality has emerged as one that appears to be the most likely to unify researchers. The Five Factor Theory has not been developed particularly with substance abuse in mind, but rather is thought to be applicable to many different areas of life. Costa and McCrae (1985) described the Five Factors as being Neuroticism, Extraversion, Openness, Agreeableness and Conscientiousness and although some researchers have taken issue with these terms, primarily because the separation of trait components may be seen as rather artificial due to their dynamic interaction, they have also received considerable support.

In addition to general personality research, there has been much specific discussion in the literature over the question of the existence or otherwise of an Addictive Personality, an identifiable personality type which definitively predisposes a person to becoming a substance addict. Some researchers appear to consider its presence a forgone conclusion whilst others regard the concept with a substantial degree of scepticism. As with many of the other theories we have looked at, the Addictive Personality is something that we might wish did actually exist. Again it is simple to understand, intuitively correct and would be easy to develop tests for. But unfortunately it is not only a simple concept, it is actually rather simplistic and although it may well make up a component of the BPS approach, it cannot, on its own explain substance abuse.

One of the reasons for this is that although traditional models of personality assume that causality flows from the trait to the behaviour with only a very weak flow from the opposite direction, if the subject population is made up of substance abusers, the question of causality is even more pertinent than if the subject population were non-pathological. Researchers have to attempt to conclude if the trait is antecedent, concurrent or consequent to the addictive behaviour. In other words it has to be considered if the anxiety state found in an amphetamine abuser was caused by the drug rather than the anxiety causing the individual to seek out amphetamine.

In spite of this continuing controversy over the Addictive Personality, it does appear possible to say that substance abusers have aspects of personality that differ in some way to non-abusers. However, the level of these differences remains unclear. In order to demonstrate just how unclear this is, Retka and Chatam said that the personality of drug addicts was:

> . . . *alienated, frustrated, aggressive, emotionally unstable, nomadic, narcissistic, dependent, sociopathic, hedonistic, childlike, paranoid, rebellious, hostile, infantile, retreatist, cyclothymic, constitutionally immoral, hysterical, neuroesthenic, self-indulgent, introspective, essentially normal . . .*

> (Retka and Chatam, 1974: 15).

Although Retka and Chatam's comments indicate that researchers have found substance addicts with numerous divergent facets to their personalities, there have also been many instants where striking commonalities have been found too, particularly within the concept of Costa and McCrae's Neuroticism. These commonalities have prompted researchers to examine this particular area of personality in detail.

The consensus of opinion among researchers is that substance abusers exhibit raised levels of Neuroticism, before, during and after addiction. This is really quite good news because if a difference exists, whether it be in personality, genetics or social factors then researchers can measure it and if measurements can be made then those at risk can be identified.

This Neuroticism is readily identifiable in pre-alcoholic children by raised incidents of nail-biting, phobias, nightmares, tantrums, tics, stuttering and other common indicators. Although the trait of being neurotic can be seen to be raised in substance abusers, it is possible that neuroticism is, by itself, too broad a concept to be particularly useful in, as politicians would say, 'real terms'. In other words saying that neuroticism is raised in substance abusers is fine in the laboratory, but is it any use outside the university campus? Neuroticism itself is made up of various sub-traits we have found as being abnormal in a substance abusing population. These are lack of self-esteem, depression, anxiety and a tendency towards a lack of self-concern (a sort of reverse hypochondria).

It can reasonably be concluded that although the Addictive Personality may not exist by itself, aspects of it are useful in the study of substance misuse. There are differences between people who misuse chemical substances and people who do not and utilised in the right way these differences can be helpful in both identifying potential misusers and those who already have substance misuse problems.

The Self-Medication Hypothesis

The Self-Medication Hypothesis is another one of those theories which seems intuitively correct. It appears obvious and neat and to a certain extent, that is exactly what it is. Unusually for theories in this area, it not only seems simple, but it actually appears to be useful, practical and possibly even right!

The Self-Medication Hypothesis was first put forward by Khantzian in 1985. Basically, he said that all people use different substances to alleviate the symptoms of an underlying, and normally undiagnosed psychiatric condition. Essentially what is being suggested is that substance abusers primarily use various different substances in order to reduce emotional suffering whilst the pleasure-seeking motives are by-products, secondary to the self-medication. In other words, by drinking to excess people are treating an illness and the sensation of getting drunk is a 'bonus' or side effect of that treatment.

Khantzian asserted that addicts made a distinct drug choice in order to medicate themselves in a way they saw appropriate to their perceived condition and that this choice was the result of the distinct properties of the drug choice interacting with the primary feeling state they were experiencing. For instance, Khantzian suggests that heroin addicts prefer opiates because of their powerful muting action on the disorganising and threatening affects of rage and aggression to which heroin users are predisposed. On the other hand, cocaine has its appeal because of its ability to temporarily raise lowered levels of self-esteem, and to relieve distress associated with depression, over-excitability and hyperactivity. Khantzian asserts that while addicts tend to experiment with many different drugs, most have a particular drug that they come back to time and time again, their 'drug of choice' and that it is the selection of this drug of choice that is at the heart of the Self-Medication Hypothesis.

It would be neat and symmetrical indeed to be able to say that people with low self-esteem use cocaine whereas persons who are aggressive use opiates. Unfortunately this does not appear to be the case as there are many other variables such as economics and availability that are not covered by the Self-Medication Hypothesis. Until further work is done the Self-Medication Hypothesis remains an attractive, but empirically unsupportable, hypothesis.

The BioPsychoSocial (BPS) Approach

At long last, and not before time, we have arrived at the BPS group of hypotheses. Although the preceding discussions have been by no means exhaustive, they have set the scene for describing the BPS approach which is the one adopted by this book.

It does not seem reasonable to argue against this point of view. As we have seen, for a very long time, doctors, psychologists and others aligned themselves with single cause theories of substance abuse, but these single factor theories simply do not hold water. Single factor theories may be attractive but they are simplistic and cannot explain complex human behaviour.

Asking a single factor to explain substance abuse is rather like saying that the only reason for increasing heart disease is the eating of chips or the only reason England keep getting beaten at cricket is because Ian Botham and David Gower have both retired. Clearly any complex condition is multi-causal and will vary from situation to situation and from person to person. In the case of the England cricket team however, it is unclear if single factor theories, multi-factor theories or anything else for that matter can explain away the problems.

As with many areas of medicine, it does appear that the various disciplines of psychology are slowly drawing together and acknowledging that each has something to offer when trying to explain the mystery of substance abuse and the addictive state. With this in mind, it is fair to say that effective, workable, BPS models may at last be emerging that are, at the very least, a useful framework on which to build.

But what is a BPS Model? As we noted in Chapter 1, it may be any one of a number of theories that draw together elements from across different disciplines. There is not any one particular BPS model, but rather numerous models that may draw together paradigms from, for instance, sociology, psychology and neurology. Commonly a BPS model may assume that an addictive state has been caused by a complex interaction of biological susceptibility, psychosocial and cultural influences, pharmacological effects and learned behaviour.

Early work on BPS models came from Ewing (1983), Tarter (1986) and Wallace (1989) and they have subsequently been refined over the years. Wallace (1993) suggests that it would be hard for any worker in the field to reject the BPS models as they are both logically and intuitively correct. He suggests that the new BPS models must be accepted because they are based on the fact that:

> . . . *biological, behavioural, cognitive, psychosocial and sociocultural events all enter into the nature of alcoholism and addictive disease of all types.*

(Wallace, 1993: 76).

But is a BPS perspective any different, in practical terms, than the older Disease Models and associated concepts? It seems fair to answer that with a qualified 'possibly'. One of the main advantages of BPS models is that they are not restrictive and allow wide exploration and interpretation across disciplines. In this way adoption of these models allows for a reduction in the ideological clashes that has characterised much of the work in this field up until now. Additionally, BPS models fit reality far better than any of the unidimensional models described earlier. We are, after all, complex beings, acted on by our biology, genetic history, social factors and so on.

To summarise: A BPS perspective of substance abuse promotes productive integration of diverse research perspectives; explains clinical heterogeneity while preserving common clinical dimensions; necessitates multidimensional assessment; and promotes matching through comprehensive, individually prescribed treatment. In other words, at the moment it works fairly well until something better comes along, but whatever that something might be, it will almost certainly not be a single entity theory, but will take an holistic approach which encompasses all aspects of peoples lives.

Conclusion

This has been a long and complex discussion. In parts, we have been forced to go against the overall philosophy of this book which is one of easy accessibility. Unfortunately it has been necessary and although many theories have been deliberately left out it is hoped that this summary has given some idea of the theoretical state of play in the substance abuse field of research.

Finally in this background section of the book we will describe roughly who is using what and where and in what quantities. Following that we will focus on the main part of this book – risk assessment.

Chapter 5

The Extent of Substance Use

Introduction

This chapter is important as understanding exactly what is going on in our society in relation to drugs and young people is at the very heart of what we are writing about. In it we will present some of the latest prevalence figures for drug and alcohol use. We discuss alcohol at some length because, as will be seen later, alcohol is a major causal factor in adolescent drug use and its role needs to be understood. We also look briefly at the relationship of substance use to tobacco smoking.

You will have gathered by now that we believe that a great deal of what has been written about drugs and their use is incorrect at best and at worst extremely damaging. This is particularly true when it comes to saying who is using what and how much they are using. Accurate knowledge of this is, however, important as everyone needs to know about the society in which their children are living and growing up.

There have been numerous scare stories in the media over the years: many of them have grossly exaggerated the problem of drug use, particularly in young people and many have given the impression that substance abuse in our society is the norm rather than the exception. Generally speaking this is not the case. Certainly there is extensive drug use, but it can be argued that excluding alcohol, there is relatively little substance *abuse*.

A classic case of scaremongering is in relation to Ecstasy. It has been widely reported that Ecstasy is an extremely toxic substance which kills easily in small doses. This is simply not the case. While we are not for one second suggesting that young people should take the drug, what we are saying is that if they do then they are not at any great risk from the substance itself. Statistically users are more likely to die from an adverse reaction to penicillin than from Ecstasy intolerance. What they are at risk from is alcohol poisoning (as excessive drinking often accompanies Ecstasy use) and also from heart failure contributed to by dehydration. This is just one example from recent times, but there are many others.

Much of the data in this book comes from my own research and focuses on the UK, but we have also drawn on work from other agencies not only in the UK, but also in the US and other western nations. Where UK figures are quoted these come from government statistics as well as from surveys carried out at the Centre for Substance Abuse Research at the University of Wales, Swansea (CSAR) and those carried out by the Schools Health Education Unit at Exeter University. European data comes from the European Monitoring centre for Drugs and Drug Addiction (EMCDDA) and American data from the National Institute on Drug Abuse (NIDA).

Many of the figures are an amalgamation of a number of studies from these organisations and are intended to refer only to western nations, principally the UK, EC member states, the USA and, to a lesser extent, Australia and New Zealand. Wherever possible we intentionally do not differentiate between geographic areas so unless otherwise stated the data will refer to all adolescents in all western societies. There are of course notable exceptions to this rule because differences do exist from country to country (for instance crack use is much higher in the UK, the reverse being true of Ecstasy).

Obviously prevalence figures are changing from day to day but for the purposes of this book, it doesn't matter much if on Tuesday 6 per cent of 15-year-olds say they are using Ecstasy once a week and on Friday that figure is 5.5 per cent. What is important is the trend and in that sense drug use statistics are like the weather. On their own the high temperatures reached are irrelevant, but if looked at in context of a general warming of the planet then they are important – it is the same with drugs, it is not particularly important if there is a blip when a certain substance becomes fashionable, but it is important if in 1950 10 per cent of children regularly used drugs compared with 20 per cent in 1980 and 30 per cent in 2000 for example.

General Background

The World Health Organisation estimates that substance abuse accounts for about 8 per cent of all deaths. However, in addition to the mortality due to substance use, a substantial amount of disability and social problems are also due to substance abuse, and in particular many of these problems can be attributed to alcohol. As a result, the true public health burden of substance use is undoubtedly several times greater than these mortality estimates suggest, which are in themselves high.

Illegal Drugs

Levels of consumption of a wide range of internationally controlled psychoactive substances (opioids, cocaine, stimulants, sedatives and hypnotics, cannabinoids and hallucinogens) are increasing in many countries. This trend is often accompanied by lower ages of initiation into use. The world production and supply of psychoactive substances continues to grow at an alarming rate. Many developing countries are now experiencing rapid increases in the use of these substances, and are also experiencing the resulting problems.

The health consequences of illicit psychoactive substance use are numerous and diverse and are not only related to the direct action of the drugs themselves, but to the mode of administration and associated life-style factors. The general poor health, social and material conditions of many users complicate the relationship between substance use and ill-health. Other confounding factors can include alcohol and tobacco use among users of other substances; involvement in sex work; exposure of drug users to violence and other harms; education; lack of access to health and welfare services. These factors can contribute to, or be, the primary cause of ill-health and disease among drug users.

Injecting drug use generally involves greater health risks than non-injecting use. In many countries drug injection is becoming increasingly common. The extent of injecting drug use is difficult to assess although there are WHO estimates which suggest that five million people currently inject drugs world-wide. Evidence from around the world also indicates that the number of injectors is rising and may well continue to do so. The number of countries reporting drug injection rose from 80 in 1989 to 121 in 1995 and this number continues to rise. Drug injection is a significant risk factor in the spread of human immunodeficiency virus (HIV), hepatitis B and C, and other blood-borne infections. The major cause of death in populations of drug injectors (other than HIV) is drug overdose. Drug overdose is poorly understood and there is no clearly established criteria for what constitutes an overdose. Variable individual tolerance to the drug and the consumption of combinations of drugs at the time of overdose are likely to be the important and complicating factors.

Stimulants, particularly amphetamines and their analogues (such as Ecstasy), are used in many regions of the world. The extent of the health risks and other problems associated with amphetamine-type stimulants are not sufficiently well understood. This lack of understanding is a major obstacle to effective preventative measures.

The deliberate inhalation of volatile solvents is also an increasing problem world-wide. These substances such as glue, petrol, paint thinners, domestic polish and aerosol sprays are particularly attractive to marginalised and vulnerable young people because of their ready availability, low cost, and the rapidity of mood alteration following inhalation. Hazards associated with their use range from sudden deaths to various neuropsychological and physical harms as well as psychological trauma.

Alcohol

Alcohol is a significant direct cause of death and disability as well as being a secondary contributor through road traffic accidents, industrial injuries, accidental drowning, homicide and suicide. As well as the problems affecting individuals, alcohol is also implicated in a range of social problems including crime, violence (particularly against women and children), marital breakdown, loss of productivity and child abuse. Although the protective effect of moderate alcohol use against heart disease has been noted in developed countries (particularly France), such beneficial effects are outweighed by its harmful effects. In developing countries the consumption of alcohol is increasing rapidly and only limited alcohol control policies and educational interventions have been developed to prevent and reduce alcohol-related harm. Irresponsible and uncontrolled advertising and promotion of alcoholic drinks in these countries are contributing to an increase in their consumption, and of course the resultant problems.

Tobacco

Although we have not been discussing tobacco much so far, it is worth mentioning it at this point. Although not central to the purpose behind this book tobacco is interesting in that its use presents another major public health problem and various aspects of its use are tied up with adolescent substance abuse. Currently, it causes about 6 per cent of all deaths. By the year 2020, on current smoking trends, tobacco is predicted to be the leading cause of disease burden in the world, causing about one in eight deaths. Most of this massive increase in mortality is expected to occur in the developing world where about half of all men are current smokers, but fortunately few women are (by the way this is not the case in the UK where there has been a huge increase in female teenage smoking). Tobacco is quickly becoming a greater cause of death and disability than any single disease. Within the next three decades, tobacco may well be responsible for more deaths than AIDS, tuberculosis and the complications of childbirth combined. However, the sheer scale of tobacco's impact on global disease burden, and particularly what is likely to happen without intervention in developing countries, is often still not fully appreciated. The risk at the individual level is even more alarming. On current evidence, 50 per cent of regular smokers who start in adolescence and continue to smoke throughout their lives will eventually be killed by tobacco, half in middle age, half in old age. Those who die before age seventy from a tobacco-related cause will lose, on average, 22 years of life expectancy. If current smoking trends persist, it is estimated that about 500 million people currently alive will eventually be killed by tobacco.

We are not going to begin preaching, but it is incredible to us that it is still not fully acknowledged by some tobacco companies that their products kill people. Also some Western governments are still prevaricating about allowing tobacco companies to advertise, often agreeing with the company's claims that their advertising is not aimed at getting young people started on cigarettes, rather being aimed at enticing established smokers away from rival brands! Scientists are sometimes criticised for being naïve, but to imagine *governments* falling for that line is beyond belief.

Adolescent Substance Use

The rest of this chapter will now concentrate on adolescent substance use and in addition to looking at levels of use. We will also look at patterns of use as well as the interaction between alcohol and drug use and we will look at how use of one substance can affect use of the others.

Key points

- Alcohol use by young people is on the increase in the UK, and abstainers are now rare. For example in 1943, 75 per cent of 7 to 14-year-olds in England had used alcohol, but by 1988 this figure had risen to 96 per cent.
- Alcohol consumption patterns are changing. Young children are using large quantities of alcohol at each drinking session. Young adolescents do not drink 'socially', they are drinking to get drunk.
- Cigarette smoking is again increasing in young people with regular smoking being a lot more common in girls than in boys.
- Boys are more likely than girls to use illegal drugs.

- Overall 45 per cent of 16–19-year-olds in the UK say that at some time or another they have used an illegal drug – 31 per cent in the past year and 19 per cent in the past month.
- Cannabis is by far the most widely used illegal drug. Following large increases in use during the late 80s and early 90s, cannabis use has now stabilised across the UK and the European Community. About 75 per cent of all illegal drug users only use cannabis.
- Amphetamines are the next most widely used drug, followed by LSD and then Ecstasy.
- Cocaine use is relatively rare, particularly amongst young people. Crack use in the UK is even rarer. The crack epidemic which was predicted ten years ago has not occurred although there are pockets of UK crack use, particularly in some inner cities.
- Opiate (heroin) use is also relatively rare and injection of heroin is even rarer.
- Adolescents do not use illegal drugs unless they also drink alcohol. Alcohol use always accompanies illegal drug use and generally precedes it.
- The heavier the alcohol use, the more likely the drinker is to use other drugs. Adolescents who prefer stronger drinks (i.e. spirits) are more likely to develop a drug problem than adolescents who prefer drinks with lower alcohol content (i.e. beer).
- 'Hard' drug users have almost always used cannabis first, but very few cannabis users go on to use hard drugs.

Illegal drugs

One of the problems with producing prevalence figures for illegal drugs is that those figures are changing day by day and are different region by region. Drugs that are popular or available in one area may not be used in another. There are a thousand and one factors which affect drug use, particularly adolescent drug use, so any book, magazine or newspaper which claims to be giving definitive figures cannot, with the best will in the world, be accurate. Also of course, any published figures are automatically out of date by the time they reach the general public. However, as we mentioned earlier, it is *trends* in drug use which are important, not short fads.

There are many prevalence studies taking place all the time and generally there are several running in the same country at the same time. Often they use different methods for gathering their numbers and, as such, it can be difficult to directly compare the figures. This is particularly true when comparing the different figures coming out of the United States and European countries including the UK. One fact is generally true however, the figures gathered usually underestimate drug use. This is because nearly all surveys into adolescent drug use (including our own) take place in schools and often the young people you most want to learn about (i.e. the drug users) are out of school when the surveys are carried out because of illness, suspension or are truanting because of reasons directly associated with drug or alcohol use.

Remember also that many of the drug prevalence figures presented to the general public have been subjected to political spin to such an extent as to make it possible to say from the same set of figures, for instance, drug use amongst 1-year-olds has been both increasing and decreasing over exactly the same period of time. This may sound ridiculous but unfortunately it is true and the way in which figures are presented largely depends on the motivation of the person presenting them. For instance, suppose that 1 per cent of 15-year-olds used heroin in 1980 and in 1995, you might think that heroin use in that age group had remained stable. But suppose someone else looked at the figures in a different way and said that in 1980 14 per cent of heroin users were aged 15 and in 1995 20 per cent of users were 15. You get the point.

A final problem is that not all figures can apply to all situations; say for instance that hypothetically 3 per cent of 16-year-olds in inner city Manchester use heroin, clearly it is unlikely to be mirrored by 16-year-olds living on the Isle of Skye. That may be a rather daft and extreme example, but you get the general idea. The figures in the tables that follow are therefore a generalisation and we will put some flesh on the bones of those figures in the commentary which follows.

What we are trying to do is cut through all the spin and hype and present a simple set of figures which tell you what proportions of young people are using what drugs.

As we said, these figures do not pretend to be particularly accurate. If we wanted to we could present you with extremely accurate figures of, say, cannabis use by 14-year-old girls in North-West London, but what would be the point? There is a lot of data available which gives this type of detail, but unless you are particularly interested in the geographic and social area where the work was done, the figures are largely irrelevant.

The numbers in these tables and in the graph below, are general figures taken from all over the Western world and clearly indicate an upward trend in drug use. These are bald and very basic figures which show without question that drug use amongst young people is on the increase.

Table 5.1a The average percentage of boys who have ever used an illegal drug

Age	1987	1988	1989	1990	1991	1992	1993	1994	1995	1996	1997	1998
11–12	1	1	1	1	2	2	3	3	2	3	4	4
12–13	2	2	2	3	4	4	6	6	7	9	9	9
13–14	3	3	4	9	12	14	16	18	18	18	18	19
14–15	5	6	7	11	19	23	27	32	33	34	36	38
15–16	8	9	12	15	28	29	30	35	36	36	39	38
16–17	9	10	15	18	30	32	33	38	38	40	42	43
17–18	10	11	16	18	31	32	34	38	40	42	42	45
Mean	5.4	6.0	8.1	10.7	18.0	19.4	21.3	24.3	24.9	26.0	27.1	27.7

Table 5.1b The average percentage of girls who have ever used an illegal drug

Age	1987	1988	1989	1990	1991	1992	1993	1994	1995	1996	1997	1998
11–12	1	1	1	1	1	1	1	1	1	1	1	1
12–13	1	1	1	1	1	1	1	2	1	2	2	2
13–14	3	3	3	4	4	5	7	8	9	10	11	11
14–15	3	4	5	10	11	14	15	20	21	22	28	27
15–16	4	5	7	9	12	15	18	20	22	26	27	28
16–17	9	8	10	11	14	16	20	21	24	28	30	32
17–18	11	12	14	18	20	24	26	28	30	33	38	40
Mean	5.4	4.6	4.9	5.9	7.7	9.0	10.9	12.6	14.3	15.4	17.4	19.6

These figures are also confirmed by other types of data too. For instance seizures of drugs by law enforcement agencies are going up as are teenage drug related consultations in hospitals. All these types of data indicate a rise in use, but we have chosen to show you the most straightforward of these based on what young people actually say they are doing.

It is clear from these numbers that illegal drug use for both boys and girls has been increasing for the past ten years or so. This increase has been slightly greater for boys than for girls, but nevertheless drug use by girls has still been going up significantly. If we look at the older end of the age range we can see that nearly half of all adolescents say they have tried drugs.

Herein lies an interesting and very important point: *'nearly half of all adolescents say they have tried drugs.'* This is a very typical figure of the sort

Figure 5.1 Average number of 11–18 year old boys and girls using drugs 1987–1998

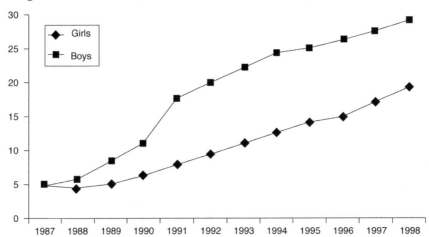

which often dominates newspaper headlines, but although startling, it can also be misleading. Clearly it should be of concern that nearly half of our young people say that they have tried drugs, but *how often* have they tried them? Smoking a single cannabis cigarette is a long way from being a regular hard drug user. Of far more interest should be the number of young people who are regular users, young people who are drug abusers rather than casual *users*.

In 1997 John Balding of the Schools Health Education Unit at Exeter University asked young people about regular use of specific drugs and found the following (see Tables 5.2a/b):

The most startling thing about these figures is that they are so low. We may think that a large number of adolescents are drug users, but very few of our young people appear to fall into that category. Obviously this is a good thing, but it should be borne in mind that although these figures are low, the overall trend is one of relentless increase in use in the latter part of this century. It should also be noted that this trend shows no sign of levelling out although other study's results seem to contradict this. There is obviously wide variance amongst drug use by young people. Regardless of differences in research outcomes and interpretation it is important to note that the results of even fairly casual drug use can be extremely damaging.

To illustrate this last point it is worth considering LSD which, as we mentioned earlier, is milligram for milligram probably the most powerful drug

Table 5.2a   Percentage of boys who say they are regular drug users

	11–12 years	12–13 years	13–14 years	14–15 years
Amphetamines	0.1	0.2	0.3	1.4
Barbiturates	0.0	0.1	0.0	0.2
Cannabis	0.7	1.1	4.0	10.3
Cocaine	0.0	0.1	0.2	0.3
Crack	0.0	0.2	0.1	0.2
Ecstasy	0.0	0.1	0.2	0.5
Hallucinogens	0.1	0.1	0.1	0.9
Heroin	0.1	0.2	0.0	0.2
Poppers	0.2	0.2	0.5	1.2
Solvents	0.1	0.1	0.2	1.1
Tranquilisers	0.0	0.0	0.0	0.4
Any of these	1.1	1.6	4.4	11.0

Table 5.2b   Percentage of girls who say they are regular drug users

	11–12 years	12–13 years	13–14 years	14–15 years
Amphetamines	0.0	0.2	0.2	1.2
Barbiturates	0.0	0.1	0.1	0.1
Cannabis	0.3	0.5	3.1	7.8
Cocaine	0.0	0.1	0.1	0.2
Crack	0.0	0.1	0.2	0.1
Ecstasy	0.0	0.0	0.1	0.5
Hallucinogens	0.1	0.1	0.1	0.5
Heroin	0.0	0.1	0.1	0.2
Poppers	0.0	0.1	0.4	0.9
Solvents	0.1	0.4	0.5	1.1
Tranquilisers	0.0	0.0	0.0	0.1
Any of these	0.5	1.0	3.7	8.8

known to us. Tolerance to LSD builds rapidly, but even so it must be remembered that a single bad LSD experience can be enough to send a person to a psychiatric hospital for years. Not for nothing has this drug earned the street name 'Acid'. It may not physically eat the brain, but it can have that type of effect on the mind.

So this picture of illegal drug use by young people is both comforting and gives rise for concern at the same time, but what is also of considerable concern is the rise in alcohol consumption by young people.

Alcohol

The reader may have gathered by now that we are not great fans of alcohol. If it were discovered for the first time today it would instantly be banned and categorised as a Class A drug alongside heroin. Unfortunately that is not going to happen, but an understanding of alcohol use by young people is vital to our understanding of their drug use. After parental drug use, adolescent alcohol drinking is one of the strongest predictors of adolescent drug use.

Unlike the previous section on illegal drug use, for the figures on adolescent alcohol consumption we will be using only UK data, predominantly figures taken from our own research at CSAR. The reason for this is that it is impossible to compare like with like when looking at the prevalence of adolescent use of alcohol. For example, how can you compare the United States where generally a person has to be 21 to buy alcohol with, say, France where teenage use of alcohol is almost compulsory? To put together any kind of prevalence figures based on these kind of social differences would be meaningless.

At CSAR we have carried out extensive work on underage drinking and we have found (along with other researchers) that underage use of alcohol is increasing. That is the bottom line, but another important fact is that when children drink they are also drinking a great deal more than they used to. Put in a slightly different way, many more children are drinking at an earlier age than they did a few years ago and these children are drinking to get drunk.

The percentage of 11–16-year-olds who say they are drinking on at least a weekly basis can be seen in Table 5.3.

Table 5.3 Adolescent drinkers

	11	12	13	14	15	16
Boys	33%	44%	58%	72%	74%	74%
Girls	28%	37%	56%	72%	82%	91%

Conclusions

Adolescent substance use can be summarised into a few of the important key points:

- Adolescent smoking is increasing.
- Adolescent drinking is increasing.
- Adolescents are now drinking to get drunk.
- Nearly half of all adolescents have tried illegal drugs at least once.
- Three-quarters of this use is of cannabis only.
- Relatively few adolescents are regular users of hard drugs.

Chapter 6

Risk Factors: What Are They?

Everyone, to a greater or lesser extent, is at risk from addiction and substance abuse.

That statement may not sit particularly comfortably with a lot of people but it is an indisputable fact and nothing to be ashamed of. To use an analogy, most adults are car drivers therefore we are all at risk of being killed in a car accident. We all think we are great drivers, but the very fact that we get behind the wheel of a car means that we are taking a gamble with our lives and so it is with substance abuse. What is questionable is how great is the risk within each individual?

In this part of the book we now get away from background and attempt to answer this question. In particular we will draw a picture of young people at risk from substance abuse and addiction and show how early warning signs can be spotted.

A word first though on ethics. Is it ethical to attempt to label ourselves and our children as potential substance abusers? If we spend time assessing whether individual young people are at risk of becoming substance abusers then it might be said that in doing so we are pre-ordaining them or rather condemning them before the fact and in doing so driving them to fulfil the prophecy we bestow upon them.

This is an interesting point, but it is an incorrect one. Once again, it is appropriate to use an analogy, this time with breast cancer. We know that some women are more at risk from this form of cancer than others. There are known risk factors including having relatives with the disease, living certain kinds of lifestyle and so on. If women are assessed at an early age of being at risk they can be monitored, or more properly can monitor themselves, throughout their lives and at the first sign of a problem do something proactively before it is too late. This is common sense and no-one objects to this approach with breast cancer so why should they with substance abuse?

We are not saying that young people should be labelled or stigmatised, but, as we said in the first chapter, if parents and young people are aware that they are more susceptible than average then they can be on their guard and can learn to watch out for warning signs in the same way as a woman with a family history of breast cancer would.

Risk Factors

First of all, what is a 'risk factor'? Within this context risk factors are the presence in a person's life of certain circumstances that put them at greater risk of developing a condition than people without those circumstances. Theoretically, once a risk factor has been identified it is possible to weight that factor and to develop an odds ratio associated with it. In this way it is possible to say that, for instance, a cigarette smoker has a 3:1 chance of having a heart attack compared to a non-smoker.

This approach to predicting disease (and in this case substance abuse) is precisely the same as that adopted by bookmakers at horse races. They weigh up all the factors for and against a horse and set the odds accordingly. For instance if Dobbin is known to hate running in the wet and it has been dry for weeks before the race the bookie may set odds of 2:1 against the horse winning. Conversely if it is raining at the time of the race then the bookie will set the odds at, say, 5:1.

We have adopted this approach as it is one of the few within the field of substance use (and indeed psychology in general) that lends itself to pragmatic useful outcomes which are readily understood by almost everyone. It cuts through the mumbo jumbo and allows us to say something along the lines of *George is five times more likely than Fred to have an alcohol problem at some time in his life because* . . .

We debated long and hard over whether to include details of how these odds ratios were worked out and in the end decided not to, largely because the process was very long and complex, not to mention boring. What we will say is that they have been computed by working on past, largely American research and through an examination of our own extensive database in the UK. It would be good if the maths had been easy, but they were not. For example, let us say that 20 per cent of young people who have a father who smokes, smoke themselves compared with 10 per cent of young people with non-smoking fathers. This seems simple, twice as many adolescents with smoking fathers smoke so the odds ratio should be 2:1. Regrettably life, and psychology in particular, is never that simple. The odds ratios used have been calculated using a statistical technique known as Binary Logistic Regression, but the less said about that the better. Rest assured though that the ratios you will see have not just been plucked out of thin air.

Not only does this risk factor approach make practical sense, but it also seems intuitively correct to say that there must be a quantifiable difference between two similar young people who both come from comparable backgrounds, one of whom develops a chemical abuse problem and the other who simply uses chemicals within the accepted social framework. The problem lies in identifying those differences and developing appropriate methods of assessment.

There has been a great deal of work during the last thirty years into risk assessment in substance abuse (most of it in America) and certain specific areas have been identified as contributing to adolescent substance abuse. Unfortunately one of the problems with this approach is that, until recently, researchers have tended to take a single factor as the focus for their research and have tried to say that their particular risk factor is the one which causes addiction.

Clearly a single factor approach is doomed to failure as it is now widely acknowledged that there is no single cause of adolescent substance abuse, but rather the condition is caused by a constellation of interacting factors. It would be marvellous if we could come up with a single factor like a dodgy gene as the root of the problem, but we cannot. Therefore, we are forced to look at the more complex options.

In addition to adolescent substance abuse being multi-causal, the presence of risk factors also has a cumulative effect with risk of substance abuse increasing with each additional factor added. For example, if we turn to the field of medicine, it is well known that cigarette smoking contributes to heart disease and, as already mentioned, it is estimated that a person who smokes is three times more likely to develop coronary heart disease than a non-smoker with normal blood pressure.

Risk factors for adolescent substance abuse are linked in a similar way, but, as with the heart disease example, not all risk factors have the same degree of influence which makes life ever more complex. The purpose of identifying individual risk factors is so that a person can address these and hopefully prevent later substance abuse problems. Risk factors for substance abuse later in life can broadly be placed in three main categories:

- **Biological**: which includes any possible genetic pre-disposition to substance abuse.
- **Psychological**: particularly factors concerned with certain aspects of personality.

- **Sociological**: which encompasses the family and peer groups, as well as secondary behaviour such as delinquency and academic standards.

Before we turn to actual risk factors themselves, it is very important to get one thing perfectly straight. Just because a person has a risk factor in their lives does not mean they will become a substance abuser. Depression is a risk factor for substance abuse but most people with depression do not use illegal drugs or drink to excess. One of the main points of this book is that substance abuse is preventable. Even if a person has ten risk factors in their life and an odds ratio saying they are fifty times more likely to become a substance abuser than a comparable neighbour, this does not mean that they will. The odds may be stacked against you, but people beat the odds every day of the week. People regularly win the main prize in lotteries and in the UK this is a 14 million to 1 shot, but it happens.

We will now discuss each of these risk areas in turn and by the end of this chapter we will have a list of the factors most likely to contribute to a person becoming a substance abuser. We will also have some idea of the relative importance of each of them.

Biological Risk Factors

This area will not be considered in any depth as, put simply, there is absolutely nothing we can do about biological risk factors if we discover them. As said at the outset, we want this book to be useful therefore what is the point in spending time going on about the DRD2 gene (or whatever) when there's nothing we can do about it? Nevertheless, it is worth having a quick look at this area as, if nothing else, it rounds out the overall picture.

A good deal of work has concentrated on the possibility of alcoholism being passed down from parent to child and there does seem to be quite a strong link. Young people of alcoholics are much more likely to be alcoholics themselves than young people of moderate drinkers (in one study it was found that 27 per cent of the adopted sons of alcoholics became alcoholics themselves compared to 6 per cent of adopted males without a biological alcoholic parent). On the surface this looks like a pretty good case for alcoholism having a genetic factor, but unfortunately it is not that simple. Much of the evidence concerned with a genetic link is seriously flawed with experiments being badly designed and so on. At the risk of sounding patronising, the arguments raging within the academic world about the validity of these experiments are complex and of little interest to anyone except academics and we do not propose to expand on them. It is

Table 6.1 Possible links between parental and offspring drinking patterns

Parents	Offspring	
Alcoholic	Alcoholic	30%
	Moderate	40%
	Abstinent	30%
Moderate	Alcoholic	5%
	Moderate	85%
	Abstinent	10%
Abstinent	Alcoholic	10%
	Moderate	50%
	Abstinent	40%

probably enough to say that there is the possibility of a genetic link, but nothing more.

However, it is worth noting the results of one study, published in 1992 (Table 6.1). These results are interesting but, as with all the risk factors under discussion, other aspects need to be considered.

Another area where biological work is going on is concerned solely with alcoholism where researchers have been looking at the role of an enzyme called aldehyde-dehydrogenase which is important in the breakdown of alcohol by the body. Some Asians lack aspects of this enzyme and alcohol consumption and alcoholism is considerably less than in many Western races. If this finding holds up then it indicates that there may be physiological reasons why some people are more prone to becoming alcoholics than others, but again, so what? Whether you do or don't have this enzyme there is precious little that can be done about it, with today's technology at least.

Psychological Risk Factors

Psychological risk factors broadly encompass the area of personality and individual personality characteristics and this is potentially a much more useful area to us than the one just discussed.

In this section we will look at five personality traits which contribute to making a person vulnerable to substance abuse:

• Low self-esteem

- Depression
- Anxiety
- Sensation seeking
- Lack of self-concern

A few years ago a lot of people were trumpeting about something called the Addictive Personality which we mentioned earlier. If you recall, it was another of those single factor theories which sought to explain substance abuse and addiction at a single stroke. It said that people were pre-disposed to becoming an alcoholic or a drug addict if they had an addictive personality. Numerous people argued endlessly about what an addictive personality actually was and eventually the concept largely fizzled out. However, in spite of the fact that the concept of a single entity addictive personality can be largely discounted, there are personality differences between substance abusers and non-abusers and it is these differences which are useful to us. Naturally these differences are not straightforward, but after many years of research and observation it is now possible to describe some areas of personality which make a person more likely to have a substance abuse problem than might otherwise be expected.

There are several aspects of personality which clumped together we have named Neurotic Susceptibility to Substance Abuse or NSSA. This may sound suspiciously like the addictive personality, but really it is just a term used for the sake of convenience and it is something made up of several very distinctive (and very measurable) areas of personality.

Low self-esteem

The most important of these areas or traits is self-esteem. It has been consistently shown that people with low levels of self-esteem are far more likely to have a substance abuse (or alcohol) problem than people with high levels. In other words, the better you feel about yourself the less likely you are to use mind altering substances to excess. This seems pretty obvious really, but it is useful to state the obvious sometimes. In this case it is helpful as self-esteem is one of the things which lends itself quite well to being measured and if we can measure it we can put an odds ratio on it. Low self-esteem is also something people can alter, but more on that later.

Depression

Clearly related to self-esteem levels is depression. Again, this is a personality trait which lends itself to assessment and it has been well established that depression is widely associated with substance abuse. As with low self-esteem this is not too surprising, but note that we are **not** talking about clinical depression which has to be medically treated (although obviously this can be a factor). We are referring to low grade depression in which a person is most of the time a little more miserable than might normally be expected, the sort of person who is generally 'down in the dumps'.

Anxiety

A third personality trait which is associated with substance abuse is anxiety. There are numerous questionnaires and psychological tests around which measure anxiety. It has been shown time and time again that people with substance abuse problems are far more likely to be clinically anxious than non-abusers. This is an area where people have a go at scientists for stating the obvious ('of course an addict is anxious, who wouldn't be? How much did it take to come up with that pearl of wisdom?'). However, what is not so obvious is that people who later go on to become drug addicts are invariably more anxious than would normally be expected *before* they become addicted. This last point is crucial to our book. The idea behind it is not to assess people with existing problems, but rather to stop a problem from developing and being able to measure a difference in people before they begin using to excess is important.

Sensation seeking

Sensation seeking is, thankfully, a straightforward concept and it has been clearly shown that it is associated with substance abuse. Basically sensation seeking is a trait shared by people such as sky divers, off piste skiers, people in the stock markets and so on. People who score highly on questionnaires which measure sensation seeking cannot tolerate boredom and constantly experiment with new activities and concepts. These individuals are more oriented towards bodily sensations and thrill seeking. They are likely to be anti-social and non-conformist compared to those who have low sensation seeking scores. So it is not surprising that they are likely to experiment first with illegal drugs and later, if other risk factors are present, to become addicted.

Lack of self-concern

The final area of personality which we want to discuss is whether there is a link between hypochondria and substance abuse. We reasoned that if people were constantly convincing themselves they were ill and were always popping off to the doctor they were more likely to take drugs then non-hypochondriacs. Wrong. What we found was exactly the opposite which, when you think about it, makes perfect sense. After a good deal of work we decided that the opposite of hypochondria was lack of self-concern. People with this trait are singularly unconcerned about their bodies, rarely exercise, eat all the wrong foods and generally don't care what they do to themselves. Again that is something which is easy to measure.

These then are the five areas of personality which go to make up the trait of Neurotic Susceptibility to Substance Abuse. All five are well founded and it is a relatively simple matter to accurately measure them and assign an odds ratio to them which we will do in the next chapter.

However, we should emphasise once again that even if you or your child are anxious, chronically depressed, have low self-esteem, like jumping out of aeroplanes and don't care much about your body, it does not follow that you will ever have a drug problem. All this means is that given the same set of circumstances you are more likely to have a problem than a person without those characteristics. What is does not mean is that you will inevitably have a problem.

Sociological Risk Factors

The area of sociological risk factors can be further sub-divided many times and they basically include anything outside the previous two areas. However, for the purposes of this book, we will focus on the most definitive factors which, fortunately, are the ones we can do something about.

In this section we will look at the following areas:
- Early initiation of substance use
- Religiosity
- Peer influence
- Delinquency
- Academic standing
- Family substance use

Of the sociological risk factors, these are the areas which most affect adolescents' substance using habits. It is entirely possible that if we had dug deep enough we would have found research showing that left handed people were more likely to use drugs than right handed people or that people who prefer cornflakes to porridge tend to get drunk more frequently, but life is complicated enough without drawing on every possible contributing factor. It is enough to look at the major areas of influence and accept the fact that every aspect of our lives is affected in some way by our environment.

A suitable analogy to this could be with ocean tides and the pull of the moon and the planets. We know that nearly all tidal effects are controlled by the gravitational effect of the moon, but theoretically Mars, Jupiter and so on also play a part, but that part is so small as to be practically insignificant. In substance abuse we know that family drinking is a very important factor and we can look at that, but is it worth taking into account which football team a person supports because that could affect substance use? Suppose that supporters of Team A drink more than supporters of Team B; If you are a Team A supporter you are therefore likely to drink more heavily than if you were a supporter of Team B because your friends do, but are these types of factors worth bothering about? No. The factors listed above are the most significant ones and these are the ones we will be discussing and measuring.

Early initiation of substance use

There is a considerable body of scientific evidence which shows that the earlier an individual begins substance use, the greater the risk that they will go on to develop an abuse problem later in life. In particular, any substance use before the age of 15 puts a person at greatly increased risk. This is a well documented finding and applies to alcohol use as well as to illegal drug use. The earlier a person begins drinking the more likely they are to have a drink problem later in life and the more likely they are to use drugs too. There is also research which has shown that the earlier a person begins to drink regularly the more likely they are to be involved in serious crime and end up in prison. This is slightly off topic but it illustrates powerfully the importance of early alcohol use.

This is a straightforward area to assess and to assign an odds ratio to because, unless a person lies, their age of initiation is a stable fact which can not alter. Practically, it is not desirable or indeed practical to stop your young people from drinking, but if you can delay onset this would be valuable.

Religiosity

Obviously being a Muslim lessens the chance of being an alcoholic in the same way as being a Rastafarian increases the chance of a person being a cannabis user, but that is not what we mean by religiosity. In our sense religiosity is simply the belief in some form of deity.

Numerous academic studies have shown that individuals with religious convictions are far less likely to use cigarettes, alcohol and drugs than those who do not have any such beliefs. Without labouring the point, it should be emphasised that we are not talking about being a member of a church or regularly attending services, we are simply talking about a person having religious beliefs.

It is actually quite interesting to speculate as to why religiosity is a protective factor against substance abuse. Obviously if you are a member of a religious group which precludes the use of alcohol or drugs you are less likely to use. However, even if you are not aligned with a formal belief system, but are a believer at whatever level, you are still less likely to use which makes one wonder if religion is a drug substitute or drugs a substitute for religion?

Peer influence

There has been a lot of research done into the question of peer influence and substance abuse and after you cut through all the usual academic squabbles a single fact emerges: peer influence is one of the most important factors in determining whether or not an adolescent will use cigarettes, drugs and alcohol.

At its most basic level you can say that if your child hangs out with a group of non-users (maybe as part of a swimming club or something like that) then they are far less likely to be substance users than if they spend their time with current users. This is another of those statements which seem so obvious as to be not worth mentioning, but peer influence is a little more complex than that. In particular some young people are a good deal more susceptible to both positive and negative influence than others. Consider the young person who moves house and has few friends at their new school, that young person is likely to welcome with open arms any peers who appear friendly. Obviously a way to attract new friends is to conform to others standards and behaviours so if the new child is approached by a group who are already drinking and smoking . . . There are many examples of that type, but the point is that children are influenced by others and some children are more susceptible to that type of pressure than others.

Additionally, in the last ten years or so it has become increasingly important for adolescents to conform. Young people are determined to be fashion clones of each other which is great for companies, but it can cause real problems if the fashion phase becomes one which involves drugs or alcohol. The majority of researchers have concluded that the influence of peers on adolescent substance use is considerable, and it is clear that any risk factor or estimation would be unwise to leave out an assessment of their influence.

Delinquency

Delinquency is one of those areas which is rather blurred and somewhat difficult to define and probably means different things to different people, but we all know, deep down inside, what constitutes delinquent behaviour. In adolescents delinquent behaviour may include everything from very precocious sexual behaviour to general rowdiness. However, within the context of this book the term will be used to describe behaviour that has caused an individual to have come into contact with the police, to have been suspended from school or to have committed criminal acts for which they have not been apprehended. When we go on to actually assess delinquent behaviour each of these areas will be included.

The evidence that substance abuse and excessive drinking go hand in hand with delinquent behaviour is so strong that if a young person is exhibiting any of these behaviours it is likely that they will also be substance users. One study in 1993 found that 90 per cent of convicted young offenders were substance users with over 50 per cent requiring drug abuse treatment. Other research has found that adolescent aggression, suspensions from school, accidents, arrests by the police, attempted suicides and pregnancies were much more prevalent among adolescents who were substance users than amongst non-users.

Academic standing

This category is something of a problem for people working in the field of adolescent substance abuse. It is a problem for all sorts of reasons, but the main one is that we know that young people who do less well at school are more likely to be substance abusers and drinkers than those who do well. Unfortunately, it is incredibly non-politically correct to say so and researchers who link substance abuse with intelligence levels tend to get into all sorts of trouble. However, schools with lower exam scores have more substance abuse problems than schools which perform well in exam league tables. An alternative might be to call them 'neighbourhood factors'.

Another problem is the chicken and egg one (psychologists call this 'direction of causality'). The question is does low academic achievement cause the young people to turn to drugs and alcohol or do they do badly at school because they are substance users?

In spite of all the problems there has been a lot of work carried out in this area and the conclusion which has emerged is that it may not be actual academic achievements which are important but how the children think they are doing. Put simply, if you have a very bright girl who is achieving high marks, but believes she is doing badly she is more likely to use drugs and alcohol to compensate than a less able girl who believes she is doing well. If you think about this it makes sense. As we discussed, self-esteem or self belief is strongly associated with substance abuse and this concept of perception of academic standing is closely linked to self-esteem.

Clearly this is one of those areas where concerned parents of young people can help them by helping them to overcome misconceptions of their abilities, but more on that later.

Family substance use

Finally in this part of the book, we come to the role of the family and the part it plays in adolescent substance abuse. The first thing to say is that the influence of the family cannot be overstated, however before we look at actual figures we need to clear up a few things.

Obviously the influence of the family is great and it is a complex area which could probably fill several good sized books by itself. There are numerous permutations of the family, (step-parents, single parents and so on) and there are an almost infinite number of variations of attitude, behaviours and philosophies which make this area a minefield. However, what we are going to focus on here, mainly because it is the most important thing as far as adolescent substance use is concerned, is family substance use. Naturally all the things mentioned above play a part, but it is family substance use which is by far and away the most important.

It is important at this point to define the term 'family'. This may seem obvious, but it is actually crucial that we understand what we are talking about here. We will be using the word 'family' to mean any person who is living in the same home as an adolescent. A child may have a natural father who is divorced from the mother and lives away from the home who has a good deal less influence than, say, a new step-father living in the house. In our context therefore, it is the people an adolescent lives with, including brothers and sisters, and comes into daily contact with who are particularly important.

In order to describe the risk factor we are going to turn to our own recent research in which we looked at the relationship between family and adolescent use in several thousand families. Basically what we found was that in homes where there was a family substance user (a user of either cigarettes, alcohol or illegal drugs) young people were nearly *nine* times as likely to be substance users themselves compared with young people who came from non-using homes. This is a fairly dramatic figure, but it fits with what we know of family relationships. If we break the figure down to individual substances we find that young people who come from illegal drug using families are twelve times as likely to use drugs themselves compared with young people from non-drug using homes. In the case of alcohol using families, young people are nine times as likely to drink alcohol and in cigarette smoking families they are twice as likely to be smokers as their counterparts from abstinent households.

These figures are simply staggering, but you might argue, not altogether surprising. Obviously a young person who sees family members drinking is more likely to be a drinker and the same goes for drugs and cigarettes. But two things are very surprising. The first is the size of the effect and the second is the fact that drinking families produce drinking young people (not surprising), but also that drinking families, even where no one uses drugs, produce drug using adolescents too, (which *is* surprising).

One thing we have yet to mention is the effect of drunkenness within a family. You will probably not be surprised to learn that the more often a family member gets drunk the more a young person is likely to get drunk and the more likely they are to smoke and take drugs.

Thus you can see from this discussion that family substance use has an enormous influence on child substance use. We well know that parents get sick and tired of being blamed for the way they bring up their children, but in this case there is a serious case to answer. When we move on to showing you how to pull all these risk factors together into something useful, family influence will obviously figure very strongly. However, before we do that a few lines on why family influence is so strong seem appropriate.

Modelling is pretty obvious and its effects are well known to psychologists (and to the public as well). If a child sees mum puffing away on a cigarette then it's OK, isn't it? You are encouraged to follow your family's lead in most things such as learning to cross the road, how to act in public and so on, so why not this too?

When we look at Attitude we can say that parental attitudes in substance abusing families will be significantly different from those found in non-using families and these attitudes are certainly contributory factors in adolescent use. In substance using families there will inevitably be a more relaxed attitude towards substance use. However we do not suggest that this culture exists to the extent that substance use is expected, or even on the surface tolerated, particularly where illegal drugs are concerned. It is possible that if this were suggested it would be greeted with protestations of denial, but it seems likely that in these families, overt substance use is the norm rather than the exception. For example, in these families it might be expected that a packet of cigarettes would routinely be left in view or a half full ashtray kept in the living room. In the same way, it might be normal practice to have one or two glasses of wine with a meal and to treat minor headaches with painkillers rather than simply waiting for it to go.

None of these practices (with the possible exception of cigarette smoking) are wrong on their own, but they add to a culture of substance use. In these families, the use of artificial substances is a normal rather than an abnormal occurrence and as such, if an adolescent were offered cigarettes, alcohol or illegal drugs it would not be a completely alien experience for them to accept.

Finally the third area of Availability is another obvious one. Clearly in families where any combination of cigarettes, alcohol or drugs are used there will be increased availability over abstinent families.

Conclusions

Some of the risk factors in substance abuse are fixed, there is nothing we can do about them. But others such as family use are not fixed and practical steps can be taken to reduce the chance of a child becoming a substance abuser.

In the next chapter we will show you how you can assess someone and by the end of it you will be able to say how likely it is that a person will have future problems and, more importantly, why.

Chapter 7

Assessing Risk

We have covered a lot of ground: we have discussed terminology, history, theories of drug abuse, prevalence and risk factors. Each one of these areas could have been covered in a great deal more depth, but as we said in the introduction, this is not a textbook and we have given you enough detail to make you relatively expert in this area. Armed with this knowledge we can now move onto one of the main purposes behind this book – assessment of risk.

Every person is at some degree of risk from substance abuse and this, of course, very much includes children and young people. Most of the time this is not due to bad parenting, it is simply a fact of life in the society in which we live.

At this point in the book we are beginning to tread on potentially very dangerous ground. Developing questionnaires and tools of assessment goes under the name of 'psychometrics' and is really quite a complex and technically difficult process. On one level anybody can throw together a questionnaire which they say will measure some aspect of our lives, but unfortunately it rarely does. Building good tests which actually measure what they are supposed to measure really is fairly hard work as they need to be rigorously tested.

Many questionnaires in popular magazines are not scientifically based, mainly concentrate on sex (how attractive you are, what sort of lover you are and so on) and are designed to sell the magazines in which they appear. In these cases they are often fairly light-hearted and done relatively tongue in cheek (at least we assume they are), which is fine. There was one a while back, which said it could tell what type of lover you were by the kind of chocolate you ate. Clearly, unless a person is totally gullible, it is obvious that you cannot do this by saying if you prefer coffee creams over Brazil nuts. There is nothing wrong with these types of 'tests' if they are completed by people in the spirit in which they are published, they are a bit of fun and fill in a few minutes on the bus, but they should not be taken too seriously (by the way, males who were good lovers apparently preferred hard centred chocolates and their female equivalents preferred soft centre – no surprise there then).

However, at times these questionnaires look at other fairly serious areas such as the chances of a person's marriage breaking up, the likelihood of being successful at work and so on. Obviously sex is not a trivial area, but the way in which the questionnaires are presented means they are probably being done largely for fun, but unfortunately these latter examples can be presented as serious well researched questionnaires when often they are not.

We do not intend to fall in to this trap and steer you down a path which leads you to thinking that young people have, say, a 90 per cent chance of becoming a drug addict in the next two weeks when nothing could be further from the truth. As we have said several times the purpose of this book is to give you the correct facts and to be genuinely useful. We could print a questionnaire which you could score, but this would be risky to the extreme. Let us explain:

At the University of Wales they have been developing a questionnaire called the Substance Abuse Susceptibility Index (SASI) which is designed to identify adolescents at risk from substance abuse as well as the reasons behind that risk. As you can imagine this has taken a great deal of work and we have tested the questionnaire extensively on many thousands of young people. The questionnaire is now accurate and does the job we designed it to do. It is also very easy for young people to complete and just as easy for administrators to score – however, it is a complex and difficult task to interpret those scores correctly and this is where the problem lies.

At times we may have seemed fairly flippant in some of the ways in which we have represented information, but we have only done this to try and enliven a potentially dry subject area. This is a serious area which warrants serious concern and we cannot justify printing well researched scientific test scores which could cause immense harm if misinterpreted. Let us suppose that we printed the whole test and it was wrongly interpreted – the consequences could be terrible. A young person could be called a high risk person when they were not or their vulnerability could be missed altogether, this is not a chance we as psychologists, and indeed parents, are prepared to take. To use an example from a different area, most people after they had read the instructions might be able to stand a friend in front of an x-ray machine, press a button and take some sort of picture, but could they accurately interpret the film, could they spot the cancer? Of course not (apologies to any radiographers or radiologists reading this, we know there is very much more to taking x-rays than 'pressing a button', but it seemed like a good example so we exercised a little poetic licence).

The fact that you have taken the trouble to read this book this far means that you are concerned about the threat substance abuse poses. This is fine but we would not insult your concern by reducing this whole exercise to little more than a pop quiz. One of the central themes of this book is that the causes of substance abuse are incredibly complex and no book such as this should ethically or morally suggest that it is capable of turning a lay concerned person into the equivalent of a doctor, psychologist or specialist teacher who has had many years of training. It cannot be done and any book or article which pretends it can is a fraud.

However, what can we do to help you? Hopefully quite a lot.

What we intend to do now is go through each of the risk factors we have identified in turn and give you some idea of their relative importance which you can apply to your own situation. You have probably done a good deal of personal application already, for instance in the previous chapter we said that children who lived in houses where cigarettes were used were twice as likely to smoke as children from non-smoking homes. How many of you have already begun to feel concerned, or even a tiny bit guilty, because there is a smoker in your home?

By the end of this chapter you will **not** be able to say that a particular young person has a 9.5:1 chance of developing a substance abuse problem because they have a biological father who is an alcoholic, low self-esteem, lack of religious beliefs and lives in a house where people get drunk on a weekly basis. That type of precise numbered assessment is the job of professionals and it is not something which lay people, however well meaning should attempt. What you will be able to say however, is that you are aware of the particular risk factors and you will be able to get a general feel if anyone is at special risk and if so, for what reasons.

In order to help you with this we will provide odds ratios in the 2:1 format discussed earlier. These ratios have been developed largely from our own research and for the purposes of this book have been deliberately made slightly vague. For instance, if a formal assessment was being made using the SASI, answer X may give a 4.3:1 risk ratio for a 14-year-old girl, but the same answer for a boy could produce a ratio of 3.2:1. We could have supplied a table to allow you to score everything more accurately in relation to the age and gender of the person you were thinking about, but, for the reasons discussed we are not going to. The odds ratios given are therefore very general, but give you an idea of the relative importance of each of these areas and in this way you will be able to say for instance that Fred has low self-esteem (3:1) which is worse than having an alcoholic father (2:1). You will be able to get a feel of what is going on around you, but that will be enough for you to act in ways which we will discuss later.

A final word of caution before we go on. We have said this before and make no apology for going over it again because it is important: whatever risk factors family members are exposed to does not mean they will develop any kind of problem. This is crucial – just because a woman has a mother with breast cancer does not mean she will also automatically get breast cancer, she should just be more aware of her increased risk, that's all. Even if children have very high odds stacked against them and it might seem like they will inevitably have a substance abuse problem they might not unless an additional trigger factor comes along to push them over the edge. It is very important to remember this.

Biological Risk Factors

When we talked about biological risk factors in the previous chapter we did not go into them too deeply because there was little of practical value we could do if we found we had them: nevertheless they are important.

If an adolescent has a biological parent of either sex who is an alcoholic or a recovering alcoholic the chances of them having alcohol problems can be put at about 2:1. In other words they are twice as likely to become an alcoholic as a comparable adolescent without an alcoholic parent. This is regardless of whether the alcoholic parent lives with the child. The risk factor is based purely on genetics and is nothing to do with social circumstance.

The same figure for a parent with a drug problem is slightly higher at about 2.5:1. The research is far less certain here, but this figure is logical given everything else we know.

Remember also that if they have a biological parent who is an alcoholic, a young person is also more likely to use drugs too, and that most children of alcoholics do not go on to become alcoholics themselves.

Psychological Risk Factors

Self-esteem

As we have said, we have formal and very accurate ways of measuring levels of self-esteem, but they are not appropriate for this exercise for all the reasons written about above. However, what you can do is draw on your own knowledge of the person you are concerned about and get the general idea as to whether or not they might have low or high levels of self-esteem. You will know this from remarks they make and, if they have very low levels, probably from other people such as their teachers. You might also like to imagine how the person would score the following statements if faced with them in a paper and pencil test which had the possible answers of Strongly Disagree, Disagree, Neither Agree nor Disagree, Agree and Strongly Agree. Think about that (or actually ask them) and it will give you the basic idea of the level of their self-esteem:

- I think my parents or carers are proud of me.
- Sometimes I think I don't deserve to be happy.
- I think that I am a good person.
- I like the way I am.

These statements are straightforward and surprisingly accurate when given as part of the SASI. When we use these and similar ones in the SASI we divide scores into one of four categories, but for our purposes a general feel of a person's level is quite enough.

Self-esteem is a very important risk factor in substance abuse, but low self-esteem can also lead to all sorts of problems in many other areas of a person's life from sexual relationships to academic achievement which of course can have a knock on effect contributing to substance abuse which is where things can get complicated.

A child with very low levels of self-esteem would have an odds ratio of between 4 and 6:1 depending on their age with older young people being more vulnerable than younger ones. Obviously the higher their self-esteem was, the further these odds ratios drop.

Depression

Depression is very common in our society and seems to be on the increase, particularly in adolescent boys and it is also strongly associated with substance abuse.

If you are wondering about a young person being depressed think about how they might respond to the following statements:

- I don't have a good appetite.
- Everything I do takes a lot of effort.
- I often wake up late in the mornings.
- Compared with others at school I always seem to be down in the dumps.

Appetite, energy levels and sleep patterns are good indicators of depression which is something that can be observed for themselves, but don't be afraid to ask a young person if they are feeling depressed. Obviously everyone gets depressed from time to time so pick your moment. Do not ask the question when it is obvious they are depressed because of a row or some traumatic event which has just occurred. Remember that you are interested in how they are generally, what is normal for them. It is people for whom depression is normal who are at particular risk.

Adolescents who are mildly depressed have an odds ratio of about 1.5:1, but young people who are very depressed a lot of the time have a ratio of 2.5:1. Remember also that depression usually goes hand in hand with self-esteem.

Anxiety

As we said earlier anxiety is a fairly good predictor of substance abuse – people use all sorts of drugs for all sorts of reasons, but whatever the reason anxiety in some form is generally noticeable in them.

It can be fairly obvious when a person is overly nervous or generally stressed out, but, as with the previous two categories, thinking about how they would respond to the following four statements might be helpful to you:

- I tend to worry about things.
- I hate being late for things like school.
- I quite often feel frightened.
- I sometimes get sudden feelings of panic.

Anxiety is not as important as self-esteem and depression, but the odds ratio for adolescents who are mildly anxious is about 1.3:1 and the odds for a highly anxious person is around the 1.6:1 mark.

Sensation seeking

Sensation seeking is quite a broad area and researchers who developed the concept broke it down into sub-areas of personality which need not concern us too much here, but it is worth noting that the sub-area most associated with substance abuse has been termed thrill seeking. When psychologists are assessing thrill seeking, using the sliding scale mentioned earlier, they pose statements such as the four following:

- I get bored very easily.
- I'd like to take up a sport such as sky diving or skiing.
- I like to try new things all the time.
- I prefer taking part in sport to watching it.

If you think that a young person is a mild sensation seeker then the odds ratio would be about 1.6:1. If you think they would score very highly then you could assign an odds ratio of around 2.1:1.

Lack of self-concern

Finally amongst psychological risk factors we come to lack of self-concern. This is actually a strong predictor and it is also one which is pretty easy to assess, particularly for insiders rather than for psychologists and other outsiders. Some of the items used in the SASI to assess this trait are:

- I am not very interested in the way my body works.
- I don't tend to worry when I get ill.
- I don't often exercise.
- If someone I know gets ill, it really bothers me.

A general knowledge of a young person is possibly of more use here than formal questions. Are they likely to take an aspirin at the first sign of a headache? Are they heavily into junk food even when they know it can be bad for them? Have they got no interest in active sport? If you talked to them about extending their life span through exercise and healthy eating do you think they would say something like 'I'd rather eat hamburgers and watch telly than eat lettuce and go running everyday just so I can live an extra year or so'.

For young people who have some concern about their general physical wellbeing, but not as much as might normally be expected, the odds ratio is around 1.8:1. However, for young people with extremely low levels of self-concern this rises considerably to 3:1.

In the case of substance abuse, being a bit of a hypochondriac is a pretty good thing, and that is it for psychological risk factors!

Sociological Risk Factors

In many ways this final category is the most important and, at the same time the most complex. It is important because the odds ratios tend to be high, but it is also important because with most of the factors there is generally something we can do to improve the odds. It is complicated because every factor is affected by every other factor which makes the setting of odds ratios a bit complicated. Nevertheless . . .

Early initiation of substance use

The earlier a person starts using substances the more at risk they are from later abuse. Regrettably this is not a sociological risk factor we can do anything about, first use is first use and once it is done it is done.

A crucial cut-off point is age 15, use before that age is serious, initiation afterwards is less so. However, let us stress that by first use we do not mean the first puff on a joint or a few sips of wine. What we are talking about here is first *regular* use which we can take to mean at least weekly use of a substance. If a 14-year-old boy once got his hands on the brandy bottle one Saturday afternoon while the parents were out shopping, drank a few glasses and was then copiously sick everywhere, apart from the mess this is not really a huge problem unless it starts happening every weekend. In a similar way if it is a social norm, for instance, to have a formal Sunday lunch where the adults share a bottle of wine and give the children half a watered down glass then this too is not a problem.

Basically with this risk factor it is a sliding scale; the earlier adolescents start the higher the odds are that they will have some sort of problem later on in life. Here are a few examples for different ages and for this we are talking about any combination of regular cigarette smoking and/or regular alcohol drinking and/or regular illegal drug use. If we split the different types of substance use, early illegal drug use is worse than early alcohol drinking which, in turn, is slightly worse than early cigarette smoking. The odds ratios refer to the chances of the child having a later problem with either alcohol or drugs:

- First regular use at age eleven 14:1.
- First regular use at age twelve 13:1.
- First regular use at age thirteen 9:1.
- First regular use at age fourteen 8:1.
- First regular use at age fifteen 7:1.
- First regular use at age sixteen 4:1.

As you can see, these are very high odds ratios and a clear pattern emerges. We will discuss practical issues later, but essentially the later you can delay regular use the better. Note the difference between ages 15 and 16 and between 12 and 13.

Current personal use

This is not something we have mentioned before, but clearly it is important and is tied up with the previous category. We do not propose to give odds ratios here because the whole area is just too complex and any figures we gave could be misleading.

The reason it is particularly difficult is because patterns of use are involved and odds ratios vary wildly depending on things such as frequency of drunkenness, types and strengths of alcohol being drunk and so on. What we can say however, is that the chances are your instincts will be correct on this one. Essentially the more alcohol that is being used the more likely a person is to have a later drugs or alcohol problem. This also of course applies to how often they are getting drunk, how much they are smoking and so on. This is one of those areas which does not need a number, or a psychologist come to that, because it is so obvious: if young people are using any type of substance to excess then beware as they may well be using others too.

But how do you know if they are using any kinds of substances? Again this is something difficult to determine, but it is a good idea to ask them. Depending on the type of relationship you have with the young person they might tell you straight out. If they do not there are obvious signs. With cigarettes you can generally smell them, which is also true, to a lesser extent with alcohol. As we said, young people who drink quite often do so to get drunk, so watch out for hangovers.

Apart from cannabis which has a very distinctive smell, early drug use is more difficult to detect. Primarily you might come across evidence of paraphernalia such as pipes, burnt silver foil and so forth. However, the most likely signs will be a change in the young person's behaviour although these too can sometimes be difficult to detect as teenagers are notoriously moody. Having said that, do not just brush off signs such as irritability, anger or anxiety. Ask yourself why the young person has suddenly become extremely difficult or why they have suddenly started sleeping late every day. In other words, look for changes. They may be perfectly normal changes, but if you suspect the use of drugs or excessive alcohol then it is worth thinking that behaviour changes may be due to substance use.

Religiosity

Religiosity is a funny one because the odds ratio is not particularly high and yet throughout the research it keeps on cropping up as being a protective factor. You will note that we used the term 'protective factor' rather than the more usual 'risk factor'. It is a *lack* of religiosity which puts a child at risk, beliefs protect them.

In our own research, which confirms work from America, we found that young people who did not believe in a god were 1.5 times as likely to be substance users than young people who did. This protective factor was even higher with young people who regularly went to church, but 1.5 is a reasonable figure to work with.

Peer influence

Although peer influence is a very complex topic in its own right it is actually quite straightforward to consider. Basically if a child's best friend is a substance user that child is far more likely to be a user than if their friend was abstinent. Having a best friend who is a user gives an odds ratio of 5.6:1. If a young person regularly hangs out with a group of three or more young people who use substances this figure rises to 7.1:1.

As the young person gets older and gets into boyfriend/girlfriend situations these odds ratios will dramatically increase. If an early sexual or pre-sexual partner is a substance user then it is almost certain that they will be mirroring their partner's using patterns.

Delinquency

Delinquency can be fairly fluid but for our purposes we have defined it as police contact, school suspension and undetected criminal acts. These three sub-areas give three separate odds ratios:
- Contact with the police 2.0:1.
- Suspension from school 2.5:1.
- Undetected criminal acts 2.3:1.

Delinquency is one of those areas where the odds ratios can obviously vary a great deal depending on severity of delinquency, but the figures just quoted give a rough guide of the relative importance of the area. Obviously if a young person has had multiple contacts with the police or multiple suspensions from school the odds ratios increase.

Academic standing

As we know, the question of academic standing is a bit of a minefield for political reasons as much as anything else. It is also difficult to quantify because there are degrees of performance, all of which affect vulnerability to substance abuse. However, if we ask young people how they perceive themselves as doing at school then it becomes more straightforward; it is what a young person believes, not what they are actually doing which is important in this context.

Young people who say they are doing fairly badly at school have an odds ratio of 1.8:1 and those who say they are doing very badly have a ratio of 2.4:1.

In other words young people who think they are doing badly are nearly two and a half times as likely to develop a substance abuse problem as those who believe they are doing well.

Family substance use

This final area is a very difficult one for either parents or professionals to assess mainly due to the enormous complexity of the whole issue. Having read the previous chapter you will know by now how powerful the influence of family substance use is.

Odds ratios are available for different combinations of family members being substance users, but it all becomes horribly complicated. For instance there is one odds ratio for a child who lives in a house where the mother smokes, but the father doesn't, another for a child who lives in a home where the father gets drunk once a week and a second adult such as a resident grandmother smokes and so on. We could list a lot of these various combinations, but that would very much go against the spirit of the book.

Importantly though, we feel that by now you will fully appreciate and understand the influence of family substance use which follows a very basic rule – The more substances a family uses the more a child will use. If you bear that in mind you can't go far wrong.

However, we will conclude this section by referring back to the figures we gave in the previous chapter in which we showed that:

- In homes where there is a family substance user, children are nearly *nine* times more likely to be substance users themselves compared with children who come from non-using homes.
- Children who come from illegal drug using families are 12 times more likely to use drugs themselves compared with children from non-drug using homes.
- In alcohol using families children are nine times more likely to drink alcohol themselves.
- In cigarette smoking families children are twice as likely to be smokers as their counterparts from abstinent households.

Finally, don't forget about the non-direct influence we mentioned, how family use of alcohol increases a young persons use of drugs.

Conclusions

The thing to remember is that often your instincts about what puts a young person at risk are probably correct. Generally it is the obvious things like family drug use, poor performance at school and so on which are problematical and maybe indicative of things to come. These may come as no great surprise, but some of the other things such as religiosity might.

You will also note that in some cases we have referred to family use possibly causing young people to *use* rather than later *abuse*. This has been done deliberately as research has not followed all the factors through to the later abuse stage. Some risk factors such as family alcoholism are known to be predictive of later adolescent alcoholism whilst others such as parental cigarette smoking indicate later child cigarette use.

If you are particularly worried about someone, get a piece of paper and write down, very roughly, what you think the odds ratios are for that person for the risk factors we have looked at. This is not a scientific exercise and it will not be accurate, mainly because it is someone else's view of a person, but it will suffice. Start by writing down all the headings and underneath write the odds ratios you have guessed at. Next sit back and have a look at those numbers – are they all similar? Have you thought that the young person is a bit depressed, therefore you have written down an odds ratio of 1.4:1? Did the lad start drinking alcohol regularly at age 16 and therefore has an odds ratio of 4:1? Once you have been through all the sections and looked at the numbers do not start adding them together or multiplying them or anything like that, just leave them there and think about them. Try to build up a picture in your head of the relative risk factors.

In the next and final chapter we will show you how to think about the scores and, importantly, what you can do about them.

Chapter 8

What To Do Now?

In this final chapter we would like to offer, not so much advice, but rather guidelines about where to go from here. The way we should do this is once again to go through each of the risk factors, but this time to offer interpretations and suggestions. Before that, here are a couple of general remarks.

1. The first thing is to say that however you now feel and however concerned you are about things: don't panic!
2. In spite of what you may have read and heard, relatively few people have serious problems with alcohol and even fewer have problems with drugs. Obviously people do get into trouble otherwise we would not be writing this book, and use is increasing. But having a child, family member or someone close to you with either a potential or actual substance abuse problem is still comparatively rare. Most people who become alcoholics and drug addicts recover to a greater or lesser degree, but the whole point of this book is that you can often help a person before drink or drugs become a problem.

Don't forget that if you are very worried a good place to start is always with your GP. However dire you believe your problem to be your GP will have heard something a lot worse a hundred times before, so don't be shy.

Biological Risk Factors

As before, we start with the least useful area – at least as far as substance abuse prevention is concerned. There will probably come a day, maybe 25 or 50 years down the track when we can do something about the genetic and biological aspects of substance abuse, but not at the moment. There are a few drugs available designed to help people through withdrawal from alcohol and illegal drugs, but as yet there is nothing we can do about having a genetic link with a substance addict.

All that we can say on this subject is that people should be aware of the fact that having an alcoholic or drug addict genetically close to them does place them at greater risk from substance abuse than might otherwise be the case. If you do have this risk factor within your family or know someone who does, simply be more aware of the dangers, watch out for the warning signs more vigilantly than usual. Try asking yourself questions such as 'Am I (or anyone else in my family) drinking more these days?' or 'Are we thinking more about where to get drugs from than we used to?' In the back of your mind remember the components of addiction we discussed earlier in Chapter 1:

1. **Tolerance:** A person needs more and more of a substance/activity to achieve the desired effect.
2. **Withdrawal:** A person suffers mental or physical torment if the substance/activity is abruptly withdrawn.
3. **Salience:** The substance/activity is at the centre of a person's life. In other words, a significant proportion of a person's time is spent in indulging in the activity or in planning ways of indulging.
4. **Craving:** A person has an intense desire to use the substance or carry out the activity in spite of adverse consequences.

If you feel that either you, a family member or someone you know are beginning to fulfil any of these criteria and there is a genetically close alcoholic or addict, then take extra care.

Psychological Risk Factors

Fortunately there is something that we can do about most of these risk factor areas although most of the time the actions we can take really are just common sense. We do not advocate chanting mantras, eating only exotic fruits or doing some weird exercise every day. A lot of the time, ways of reducing the odds ratios of the Psychological Risk factors are pretty simple.

Self-esteem

Perhaps we should have posed the question earlier, but what exactly is self-esteem? In very broad terms it is a person's sense of respect for themselves and the status, recognition, social success and so on which they get from people important to them. When low self-esteem is present, people, especially young adolescents, feel inferior, helpless, discouraged and lack sufficient confidence to cope with problems. These young people tend to be pessimistic, don't join in with the large group activities and are overly sensitive to criticism. And, as we have seen, these people are also susceptible to substance abuse too.

Figure 8.1

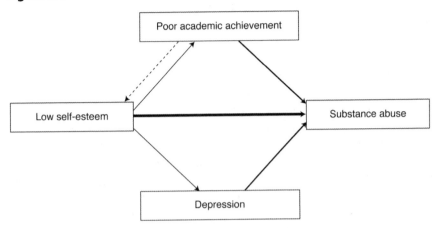

Self-esteem also affects many other aspects of our lives which in turn affect substance use. Figure 8.1 illustrates, in a very crude way the effect low self-esteem can have. The heavier the lines and arrows the more important the factor is.

We should stress straight away that this is a gross over-simplification of a very complex relationship. There is a statistical technique called structural equation modelling which draws figures like this and if this one had been done with SEM it would have looked as though it had been drawn by a pair of demented spiders on speed. However, the Figure 8.1 gets the point across that self-esteem affects other things besides substance abuse. If low self-esteem partly causes substance abuse and also partly causes poor academic achievement which in itself partly causes substance abuse then low self-esteem is, in effect, delivering a double whammy. If a child or young person has very low self-esteem, why is this and what can be done? The second question is directly related to the first. There is no point in curing the symptoms if you do not bother looking at the cause. You might be able to bolster their self-esteem, but what is the point if it is only going to go down again?

Naturally the causes of low self-esteem are numerous and many of them will be very deep-seated and inaccessible without expert help. However some will be fairly obvious. First off, ask lots of questions about their family:

- Is a step-parent getting on with your kids?
- Is there a new baby so that older children are getting less attention?

- How are they getting on with their boyfriend or girlfriend?
- How are they doing in sporting activities?
- Have they filled out any of those survey questionnaires in the teen magazines and what did they say about themselves?
- Have their school marks changed for the worse?
- Have they got many friends at school?

Ask them about their body image: young people are very keen to conform these days and part of that means having a figure or face identical to the one in the latest teen magazine. This can be extremely difficult, and possibly even embarrassing, but try to reassure them about their breast size or shape or the position of their eyes or whatever. Without going on another crusade there is some very damaging material being published at the moment and this need to conform to some fashion editor's idea of how you should look is damaging young people's self-esteem.

Obviously the best thing is to come right out and talk to your child, try to find out if they have low self-esteem by asking them, but look for less obvious signs too.

You will have noted that on the diagram above there is one dotted line which leads from poor academic achievement back to self-esteem. Most of these causal factors are two-way and you might find that a sudden dip in school performance is affecting a young person's self-esteem which is re-bounding back to lower school marks and so on.

If you identify half a dozen possible causes of the low self-esteem you are worried about, it might be a good idea to draw a rough diagram similar to the one above with self-esteem in a box on the right and all the suspicious factors elsewhere. These kinds of visual aids are quite good for focusing the mind and clarifying things for a lot of people, including the young person.

What can you do about the situation? Naturally that depends on what the factors are. Most of the time common sense will give you the answer to this question, but the most important fact by a long way is that you have identified a problem – someone has low self-esteem and is therefore at some risk from substance abuse.

Often simply knowing about a cause is enough to alter behaviours which will almost automatically put things right. Try to help them with their homework if they are falling behind at school, this will build up their confidence and therefore their self-esteem. Often young people just need kick-starting and once they have begun to improve they will do so on their own.

Having low self-esteem is very difficult for a young person and not just because it places someone at greater risk from substance abuse so anything that you can do to raise it is good. If you really feel that a young person's self-esteem is at rock bottom then you may have to seek advice. However, the most important thing is to talk to the person you are concerned about – show them that you are concerned and make sure that they know you care about them and are there to help. If you do this, then providing there is nothing seriously wrong, you should be able to lift their self-esteem and in doing so lower their odds ratio and lessen the chances of them having a substance abuse problem later in life.

Depression

Much of what we have just been discussing applies equally to depression but with one major difference: depression can be a serious medical condition which requires expert treatment.

Depression is basically caused by a chemical imbalance in the brain which in itself can be caused by all sorts of events, both physical and mental. If you suspect that someone is seriously depressed then get them to a GP as soon as possible. A GP has many ways to help. Without being alarmist remember that over the past few years every day in the UK, five young men under the age of 24 kill themselves. Suicide is the second most common cause of death for this age group in Britain today so please do not take serious depression lightly. It is a medical condition just like flu or chicken pox and can be treated very effectively by experts.

However, we pointed out earlier that in this context when we talk about depression here we are not talking about this severe acute form, but rather the underlying 'down in the dumps' type of depression. In point of fact although less severe in the short term this type of underlying depression is much more difficult to do anything about. Some people just seem to be naturally slightly lower in mood than most other people around them.

As with low self-esteem, look for changes in lifestyle, family composition, financial status and so on. If you can find some underlying cause to the change in mood then you can address that cause, but remember to look again at self-esteem as it will almost certainly be linked to this new mood.

Once again there is never any harm in asking a person why they feel the way they do. If they are one of those people who is going to abuse drugs or alcohol in an effort to raise their mood levels, try to get them to do it some other way first. As we found out in Chapter 3 a lot of illegal drugs, and alcohol in particular, are central nervous system depressants so in the long run taking them will only make things worse.

This again is a very tricky area because often adolescents' emotions are all over the place anyway as the hormones kick in. So be careful in interpreting changing emotions as indicative of drug or alcohol use – the chances are that these emotional swings are entirely natural.

Anxiety

As with depression, anxiety is a state where some people simply seem to operate on a more fired up level than others. Some people are just naturally anxious and there is probably not a lot we can do about that. What we can do something about though is where a person changes from being a fairly calm individual to being someone who is obviously very stressed out. Again causes must be looked for in exactly the same way as before, and again you must ask yourself the central question, is the anxiety being caused by drugs and alcohol. But be careful, bulls and china shops come instantly to mind. Falsely accusing an adolescent of something like drug abuse is not going to do relationships much good.

Quite often anxiety is linked to depression and in fact there's a psychiatric condition termed 'anxiety depression'. What this means therefore is that you have to look at the whole life of the person you are concerned about for clues as to why they are behaving the way they are and keep asking yourself questions. It really is a bit like being a detective.

Sensation seeking

We are going to say very little about sensation seeking, after all why should you want to do anything about this personality trait? If humans didn't have at least some degree of thrill seeking within them then we wouldn't have any mountaineers, astronauts or probably scientists either.

There is nothing wrong with being a thrill seeker providing it is kept within limits. Anything which is taken to excess is going to cause problems, but in this context if you find that a child would score high on sensation seeking scales then just accept it and be aware that it can be a contributory factor in substance abuse.

Lack of self-concern

Finally, in this section we come to something which is actually quite an important factor and it can be addressed. This can be best done by example.

It will not work if you just sit your couch potato burger-munching child down for a 'serious chat'. You can tell them until you are blue in the face about their body being the only one they've got, about it being the temple of the soul and so on. None of this will work. We do not really know why some people are hypochondriacs and others the reverse, it is one of those things where we have to accept that this is the way people are.

We suggest that one of the best ways in which to instil a healthy piece of self-concern into children and young people is to show them exactly what their bodies are capable of. It has been speculated that in years to come we will evolve into beings with very spindly legs, huge bottoms and large heads because we would be spending all our time in front of a computer or TV screen. This is possible, but at the moment our bodies are capable of much more so we need to use them. Young people need to be shown that not abusing their bodies can make them feel generally better and that by taking better care of themselves they will appeal more to others, especially the opposite sex. Lack of self-concern is leading not only to substance abuse but also to obesity and heart disease. Unfortunately, money and time become issues here. Trying to get a reluctant adolescent away from the TV and into doing something which can show them how good it can be to use their bodies can be difficult and often expensive.

We will leave it to your imagination as to how you can best motivate a young person. It seems to us that the best way to get people to realise that it is damaging to swallow pills, smoke cigarettes or drink large amounts of alcohol is not to show them the harm it can do. Showing rotting lungs in jars does not work as all young people believe they are immortal, it has been tried and it always fails. Instead, take the opposite approach and show them what their bodies could do if they were fit.

Sociological Risk Factors

Sociological risk factors are serious but often we can deal with them.

Early initiation of substance use

There was some unconfirmed research carried out in the north of the UK which showed that boys from Muslim families were virtually teetotal (as you might expect) up until the age of between 18 and 20. At that age many of the boys began to use alcohol and drugs much like their non-Muslim counterparts. These new drinkers then began to have similar problems to young people who had started using drink and drugs at an earlier age, but they did so about five years later. What makes this work even more interesting is that we know from other research that the later you can delay the onset of problematic drinking or drug use the less severe that substance abuse is likely to be. Also, and this does not apply so much to alcohol drinkers, most medium to heavy drug users give up by their mid-thirties.

This now brings us onto the benefits of delaying the initiation of regular substance use. If young people are prone to substance abuse and if it is possible to delay the onset of regular use by a few years then you are doing a very great service as the abuse will probably be far less severe and last for a much shorter length of time than if they started in their mid-teens.

We have emphasised this point because it is probably the most important one in the whole book.

Many people are fairly resigned to young people drinking regularly at an earlier age than they should, after all they will begin legally at 18. So what difference can a couple of years make? The answer is that it can make a very great difference particularly if it is not 'a couple of years', but three, four or even five.

One of the biggest problems is that biologically and emotionally young teenagers are very much still children in spite of what some parts of society might like us to think. They are not mentally equipped to handle pumping very powerful drugs into their systems day in day out: early drinking is very damaging physically, mentally and emotionally. In America you cannot drink until you are 21 and in the UK it is 18. These laws have been made because governments believe that people any younger simply cannot handle it and they are correct. The Americans have probably got it about right in this instance. As you get older you have more insight, you are more mature and taking dangerous drugs is generally safer.

The problem is that parents and those working with young people are really up against it from two fronts; firstly immaturity and secondly commercial pressures:
1. For many different reasons children are growing up faster these days, not biologically, but socially. One reason for this is that they are far more knowledgeable, for instance at 12 most not only know about reproduction they also probably know about paedophiles, various perversions and gang rape too. Did you know about gang rape when you were 12? Almost certainly not. The point of this is that children know about alcohol, they know about drugs, they know the street names, they know some of the effects, they see drinking and drug use on television and they want to do what they are convinced everyone else is doing. This is completely understandable, but many of these young people are simply too young.

However, we have to live in reality and we cannot cocoon our children forever, but perhaps we can protect them for just a little longer?

2. Young people will try very hard to make this difficult for us, partly because of what they perceive as social pressure and partly because of the commercial pressures. We are going to have to be very careful here because we do not want to fall foul of Doberman, Doberman and Rottweiller, Solicitors Ltd, however . . . Young people are under enormous pressures not only from within themselves, but from commerce too. It is a cliché, but we do live in a consumer society and we are constantly being pressured to buy, buy, buy, and that applies to alcohol as much as to clothes and CDs.

Alcohol is a very unpleasant substance to drink. Sometime ago a scientist was looking at the effect of alcohol on rats, but he could not do his work as the rats refused to drink the alcohol until he added a lot of sugared water. Give children a pint of bitter and they will not be able to drink it either, because it's too near its natural state, you really have to work at downing a pint at first. However, if you fiddle around with it a bit it becomes more palatable. Do you remember snowballs? Do you remember rum and blacks? Do you remember vodka and orange? These were all drinks which were very popular in the 1960s, 1970s and 1980s amongst young people (often girls) because they masked the taste of alcohol and made it easier to take. Macho boys of course had to force down the pints, but that is another story.

This is no longer a problem. As you know, in the UK over the last few years we have had the introduction of Alco-pops: very strong, relatively cheap sweet drinks that are easy to drink and have colourful labels with names such as Loaded and Blitzed. These drinks have overcome the problems of raw alcohol and if you drink one you hardly realise you are drinking alcohol at all, until you try to stand up that is. Generally they have about two and a half times more alcohol in them than the average pint of beer.

There has also been another 'advance', an alcoholic milk called Alco-Moo is now being sold in the UK in chocolate, strawberry and banana flavours. The companies involved with selling Alco-pops and Moo strongly deny targeting under-age drinkers, insisting that the drinks are aimed at adults. You can just imagine the scrum-half of the local rugby team going up to the bar and asking for 'a pint of lager please, half of chocolate Moo and two strawberry Moo and cokes'.

We offer you these facts without comment and leave you to make up your own minds as to who is being targeted by whom.

This all goes to illustrate the problems you are going to face when trying to dissuade young people from beginning regular substance use too early: pressure from the young people and indirect pressure from commerce via young people. Hopefully, though, we have managed to convince you that it is worth the aggravation to delay onset by a few years. If so, how are you going to go about it? Very, very carefully is the answer.

Governments, education authorities, health authorities and various other bodies have been trying for years to stop adolescents from taking up substance use, but through no fault of their own all have failed. They have failed in part because commerce spends several hundreds of millions of whatever currency you might choose to name every year promoting their products (although not to children naturally) and partly because young people believe they are immortal and none of what they are told applies to them personally. We know that anti-substance education programmes are failing because of the increases we talked about in Chapter 5. We are not having a go at the people delivering these programmes, they face an almost impossible task.

Just about everything has been tried. Policemen have gone to schools, and children have been shown the inside of prisons: it does not work. Doctors have shown films of people dying of lung cancer, but still smoking is increasing. If you watch someone coughing up great chunks of their insides and then dying in agony, how can you go outside and light up in the playground? Children do.

The only thing which has ever been shown to work is bribery. In the US a few years ago a psychologist found about a hundred cocaine addicts and paid them around $1,000 each to give up for a few weeks, about 90 per cent of them did. Unfortunately they all took it up again once they stopped being paid.

So, if governments have failed so badly what chance do you stand in the face of the huge personal and commercial pressures we have been discussing? Hopefully you stand quite a good chance as the reason for this is simple.

All drug education in schools and elsewhere is aimed at a 'mass market', by definition it cannot take into account individual differences, you can. You know the young people, you know what makes them tick, you know their strengths and weaknesses, make them work for you. Also you now know a good deal more about drugs and alcohol than most people. Although this book has not gone particularly deeply into the area, it has equipped you with enough knowledge to help. Use that knowledge to talk to young people and use the knowledge you have of a young person's risk factors to try to delay the onset of regular drinking or drug use.

Remember not to try and turn young people into teetotallers (either drink or drugs) this is unrealistic in today's world and you will lose credibility if you try and this will hinder you a great deal.

One final note before we move on: you remember that psychologist in America who successfully bribed the cocaine users? Is this a possible route for you? An average adult smoker spends about £1,000 a year on cigarettes which gives food for thought, but this is a very personal issue, something that only you can decide about.

Good luck with this one, it is important.

Current personal use

Current personal use is very much like the previous section except it is slightly further down the path of a person's substance using career. However, if you discover by whatever means that a young person is drinking alcohol or using drugs, the best strategy may well be something called harm reduction. This is a pragmatic approach widely used by more enlightened governments and individuals. Basically we have a young user (of alcohol or drugs) and that is unfortunate. They are probably not going to stop whatever we do, so let us minimise the damage being done: let us stop them turning from a *user* to an *abuser*.

If you discover a young person is using do not hit the roof: it won't achieve anything, in fact it will only make matters worse. First off, remember that you have not failed if you find a young person is using alcohol or drugs. People have been doing this ever since humans walked upright and it is perfectly normal: nearly everyone does it to some extent. They might have started a bit early, but never mind, what is done is done and now you have to deal with the situation as it is.

Remember that you are now in a far better position than most people because you have knowledge and knowledge is a powerful force. If you have carried out one of the risk assessment exercises then you will probably have a fairly clear idea as to some of the reasons behind their using, but at this stage reasons for use is probably not hugely important. What is important is to try to find out a bit more about their using: what they are using, how much and how often. If they are drinking, this will probably be fairly easy, if they are using drugs less so.

We said that knowledge is a powerful force and once you have found that a young person is drinking or using drugs it might be a good idea to pass on some of that knowledge. The problem is that young people will almost certainly think they know more than you do. However, these days young people have a great deal of information about many different subjects, but unfortunately much of it is wrong. The information you now have is correct, make sure the young person understands that.

It is essential that you are realistic at this point. Research indicates that very few young people will give up alcohol drinking once they have started, although some may stop using illegal drugs. Given that this is the case you need to work with a young person on that basis. Young people tend to respond quite well to being given some responsibility, being treated like adults. If you treat them like little children then that is how they will respond and although that may be alright for some things it is not how you want them to respond to this situation. They are exhibiting an adult behaviour and it needs to be dealt with in an adult way.

It is extremely important to make yourself accessible: that means that they know they can come and talk to you if they want to and be taken seriously. Communication is the key in this situation and without it problems can arise. What is communication? It is probably easier to say what it is not rather than what it is. Communication is not telling young people that they won't use alcohol or drugs, it is not telling them that they are grounded or that they must change friends etc. In other words, it is not about giving orders. Communication is about working out a plan of action *with* young people, not telling them what the plan is you have decided on. If all this sounds a bit 'tree huggy', then so be it, but this type of approach is far more likely to work than the authoritarian one.

What you need to do is set limits, reasonable limits decided upon with young people. There is no way in the world that you should encourage any kind of substance use, but you can minimise use by setting agreed limits. It might be said that allowing a young person to use in this situation is condoning an activity which is both harmful and also breaks the law. This is a valid point, but if you forbid them to use they are going to use anyway, but in a secretive and ultimately more destructive way than if they did it in consultation with you.

In spite of what a lot of people think, young people can be quite sensible at times, particularly if they are given the chance to be so. Most young people know that these days it is important to leave school with a good exam result, or an interesting job and they will also know that their chances of achieving this will be dramatically reduced if they have constant hangovers or are stoned a lot of the time.

This is where negotiations might come in and, again, this is something for individuals to decide taking into account all the other factors in their lives. You do not want young people to change from being casual substance users to abusers so be realistic. Compromise a little and make sure that young people are aware of the dangers of alcohol and substance use and try to steer them from being young adolescents tinkering around with substance use to responsible, mature drinkers who are not causing problems for themselves or society.

Finally in this section, you might like to think of substance use in the same light as crossing the road. Crossing the road is a potentially dangerous activity, normally it is pretty safe, but children are killed and injured every day doing it. When they are growing up you would not suddenly expect children to begin crossing the road safely on their own would you? No, of course not, you would teach them how to do it in a safe and proper manner which minimises the danger to themselves.

Having to cross roads is a fact of life in our society, so is substance use.

Religiosity

Religiosity is an area in which we both can and cannot do anything to lower the odds ratios. Most religious children come from religious families, some might say that religious parents actually force their children through both passive and active indoctrination to become religious so that in a sense parents can do something to lower the odds ratios although we will make no comment about the morality of that approach. On the other hand, as we said earlier, religiosity as a protective factor is not really about attending church so much as believing. A young person can go to a place of worship and still not be a believer just as they can believe without going to church and there is very little you can do about it.

Peer influence, delinquency and academic standing

We have put these categories together as in real life they tend to go hand in hand and it is silly trying to discuss them in isolation from each other. Friends influence delinquency which is tied up with academic achievement and expectations and so on.

To a certain extent peer influence is similar to current substance use. You cannot choose adolescent's friends, much as you might like to, and if you try and dissuade them from associating with an individual or group they will probably do it even more. Remember that saying about bulls and china shops, it applies rather well here. Peer influence is a powerful force in substance use and, frustratingly, it is one of those areas where we have little control. It also affects their schoolwork as well as their 'extra-curricular' activities which hopefully will not involve the police, but might, so what can you do if a young person is associating with those you do not like or suspect are substance users? If you are worried about their friends, their schoolwork and so on, you really have to try and look at the big picture. Without labouring the point too much, as with all these things, you have to look at a young person's actions not in isolation, but in light of everything else you know about them.

As an example, you might believe that a young person has particularly low self-esteem because they are very socially awkward and have drifted towards their current friends out of desperation. These friends are a bad influence on a young person and their academic work is slipping as a result which in turn leads to the teachers having a go at them in class so their self-esteem drops which leads them back to their undesirable friends. You have to build up this kind of picture of their life before you can decide what you can do.

As with drinking, you are not going to stop them from hanging out with friends just by laying down the law. What you are going to have to do is to provide some alternatives, after all if they are having a good time with their friends why should they stop? Help them to find new friends, something else to do, something which is even better than whatever they are getting up to with their present friends. This may well not be easy.

The other thing you can do of course, is to ask for help. There is a lot of help out there for people who want it, but many people, for numerous reasons, simply do not seek it out. If you are worried about school issues, go to the school. If a young person has had contact with the police ask the police what they suggest you do about it. Ask for help, it is nothing to be ashamed of. The chances are that people will respect you far more if you go to them asking for help and admitting that you are getting a bit out of your depth than if you just try to deny that anything is wrong and muddle through or cover up.

We are well aware that we have not said too much which is concrete in this section and this is mainly because each situation is unique and it is difficult to make specific suggestions with this kind of thing. You will have gathered by now that we are not trying to pretend we have a magic wand, we believe that this is a difficult area to work in and trying to give specific advice would be stupid.

Three things to remember though:

1. Assess the situation and take stock.
2. Communicate.
3. Don't be afraid to ask for help.

Family substance use

You saw earlier how influential family substance use is and there is something very simple you can do to decrease the risk of it to your child.

As we have said on various occasions, we are trying to be very realistic in this book and we accept that stopping family substance use is not really an option. In point of fact it is not even particularly desirable. Probably 95 per cent of households in the western world have at least one person who is some sort of substance user so to come from an abstinent family is abnormal and as we know, children do not want to be different. Also we are not suggesting that family substance use is wrong, it is not, in fact it is perfectly normal. People do things such as drinking because they enjoy it so why should they stop? Simply put, they should not. What they should do is be careful about levels of use.

The more people around them use the more young people will use too. This is a very simple and very straightforward equation. If there is someone who gets drunk three times a week then the young person will get drunk far more often than where there is a family member who gets drunk once a week, monthly or only at Christmas.

The only case where we are going to suggest abstinence is with smoking. Smoking has the following effects:

- It kills the smoker.
- It helps to kill others (i.e. children) through passive smoking.
- It makes it much more likely that others in the house will take up smoking and therefore kill themselves.
- It contributes to the recent increase in child asthma.
- If it doesn't kill then it *will* make you less fit and reduce the quality of life.
- It costs a 'packet a day person' at least £1,000 per year.
- It smells and is generally antisocial.

We make no apologies for preaching on this issue as it is important although some might say that it is a gross generalisation. Unlike drinking and certain kinds of drugs, smoking fulfils no useful functions. You do not get a buzz out of it, you do not feel relaxed, it does not make it easier to talk to members of the opposite sex, and it does not help you sit around putting the world to rights, in fact smoking does not actually do anything for you. Tobacco is just an addictive drug which has been marketed rather well over the years. You can make a good case for moderate drinking and selective drug use which is fun and no bad thing, but we cannot think of a single factor in favour of smoking. It is a wholly destructive activity.

We have studiously avoided trying to place the blame for adolescent substance use on the shoulders of anyone, but in the case of cigarette smoking then it is.

Realistically most households will contain drinkers and maybe drug users. However, consider this, two sets of fathers are worried about their young person's substance use so they both decide to sit little Susan or Johnny down for a chat. One father has a pint of lager in his right hand and a spliff in his left; the other father doesn't and both then proceed to talk about the dangers of substance use. Which parent do you think will be more successful? This is actually a bit of a trick question as the outcome of the chat will depend more on what is said, the tone of voice used and the attitude of the parent rather than whether the parent is drinking and smoking a spliff or not.

The reason for making this rather contrived point is that substance use is probably not so important providing it is at a reasonable level in the open, discussed and understood. The spliff smoking father cannot preach absti-nence, it would be just daft, but he can probably talk to his curious child about the dangers, the law, the implications of using cannabis and so on. In fact the young person will probably take far more notice of that father than the one who screams at his child about the evils of reefer madness, how one toke will instantly lead to heroin addiction and suchlike.

You can of course see where this is leading. Once again, it all comes down to communicating in a knowledgeable and reasoned way, understanding young people and understanding the social world they live in. It is about treating young people like intelligent human beings capable of making informed decisions. Good decisions which you can guide them towards.

Hopefully by now you know enough to tackle the problems of adolescent substance use with a reasonable degree of confidence.

Postscript

And so we come to the end of this book. It is very much hoped that we have managed to take a difficult subject area and make it, if not particularly enjoyable to read, then at least helpful. In some places reading it has probably been a bit heavy going (as has writing it), but we hope that we have managed to make it down to earth enough to be useful.

Because there are so many different forces at work, the causes of substance abuse are an extremely difficult area intellectually to understand, but possibly more importantly, the topic is also a difficult one to handle emotionally. We are very much aware of the image many people have of drug addicted kids lying around in filthy squats riddled with disease. That is the way substance abuse victims are typically portrayed, but please believe us when we say that statistically this is a very rare occurrence indeed. If you encounter a substance abuse problem the chances are that it will be nowhere near as bad as that stereotype and, even if the worst came to the worst, there are many agencies out there who are extremely skilled at helping victims of substance abuse.

Having said that, it is our belief that it is so much better to avoid substance abuse in the first place and we very much hope that this book may go some way towards helping you do that.

Personal Bibliography

Refereed Journal Articles

Griffiths, M.D. and Sutherland, I. (1998) Adolescent Gambling and Drug Use. *Journal of Community and Applied Social Psychology.* 8: 423–7.

Sutherland, I. (1997) The Development and Application of a Questionnaire to Assess the Changing Personalities of Substance Addicts During the First Year of Recovery. *Journal of Clinical Psychology.* 53: 3, 1–9.

Sutherland, I. and Shepherd, J.P. (2001) Social Dimensions of Adolescent Substance Use. *Addiction.* 96: 3, 445–58.

Sutherland, I. and Shepherd, J.P. (2001) Substance Use Seems to be Increasing Among 11-Year-Olds. *British Medical Journal.* 321: 1161.

Sutherland, I. and Shepherd, J.P. (2001) The Prevalence of Alcohol, Cigarette and Illicit Drug Use in a Stratified Sample of English Adolescents. *Addiction.* 96: 4, 637–40.

Sutherland, I. and Shepherd, J.P. (2002) A Personality Based Model of Adolescent Violence. *British Journal of Criminology.* 42: 2, 433–41.

Sutherland, I. and Shepherd, J.P. (2002) Adolescents' Beliefs About Future Substance Use: A Comparison of Current Users and Non-Users of Cigarettes, Alcohol and Illicit Drugs. *Journal of Adolescence.* 25: 2, 169–81.

Sutherland, I. and Shepherd, J.P. (2002) The Development of a Psychometric Questionnaire Designed to Differentiate Between Adolescent Users and Non-Users of Tobacco, Alcohol and Illicit Drugs. *British Journal of Health Psychology.* (In revision).

Sutherland, I. and Willner, P. (1998a) Patterns of Substance Use Among English Adolescents. *Addiction.* 93: 8, 1199–208.

Sutherland, I. and Willner, P. (1998b) The Influence of Household Substance Use on Children's Later Cigarette, Alcohol and Drug Use: A Three Factor Model. *Early Child Development and Care.* 141: 111–26.

Sutherland, I., Sivarajasingam, V. and Shepherd, J.P. (2002) Recording of Community Violence by Medical and Police Services. *Iniury Prevention.* 8: 2.

Willner, P., Hart, K., Binmore, J., Cavendish, M., Dunphy, E. and Sutherland, I. (2000) Alcohol Sales to Underage Adolescents: An Unobtrusive Observational Field Study and Evaluation of a Police Intervention. *Addiction.* 95: 9, 1373–88.

Willner, R., Sutherland, I. and Hart, K. (2000) Adolescents' Reports of Their Illicit Alcohol Purchases. *Education, Policy and Prevention.* 8: 3, 233–42.

Non-Refereed Journal Articles

Griffiths, M.D., Wood, R. and Sutherland, I. (1998) Adolescent Gambling: Still a Cause for Concern. *Society for the Study of Gambling Bulletin.* 32: 30–7.

Sutherland, I. (1996) Adolescent Substances Abusers: Is it Possible for Psychologists to Relate to Them? *Substance Misuse Bulletin.* 10: 1, 5–6.

Sutherland, I. (1997) Are There Identifiable Causal Factors to Problem Drinking? *Alcohol Alert.* 1: 18–9.

Sutherland, I. (1997) Star Trek: Just a TV Programme or Something Worthy of Further Study? *NPRA Newsletter.* March.

Sutherland, I. (1997) The Plight of the Mature Student. *The Times Higher Educational Supplement.* September 5, 13.

Sutherland, I. (1997) The Threat to Children From 'Alco-pops'. *The Times,* April 15, 19.

Sutherland, I. (1999) The Assessment of an Individual's Risk From Substance Abuse. *Assessment Matters,* http://www.assessment-matters.org. uk/focus/focus.htm.

Sutherland, I. and Shepherd, J.P. (2000) Adolescent Substance Use: A Possible Resurgence by 11-Year Olds. *British Medical Journal.* Www.bmj.com/cgi/eletters/320/7248/1536/a#EL2.

Book Reviews

Sutherland, I. (2001) Agenda: Ecstasy, Heroin, Cocaine. *British Medical Journal.* 321: 1537.

Conference Papers

Griffiths, M.D. and Sutherland, I. (1998) *Illegal Adolescent Gambling and its Relationship to Tobacco, Alcohol and Other Drugs.* The Twelfth National Conference on Problem Gambling. Las Vegas.

Griffiths, M.D. and Sutherland, I. (1998) *Illegal Adolescent Gambling and its Relationship to Tobacco, Alcohol and Other Drugs.* The Third European Association for the Study of Gambling Conference, Munich.

Griffiths, M.D., Sutherland, I., Wood, R. and Barons, C. (1997) *Adolescent Scratch Card Gambling in the United Kingdom.* 10th International Conference on Gambling and Risk Taking, Montreal.

Griffiths, M.D., Wood, R. and Sutherland, I. (1998, May) *Adolescent Gambling: Still a Cause for Concern.* Invited Paper, The Society for the Study of Gambling. London.

Griffiths, M.D., Wood, R. and Sutherland, I. (1999) *Underage Players' Behaviour and Problems: The Impact of Gambling on Society.* Invited Paper Presented at The European Lottery University Seminar. Heriot-Watt University, Edinburgh.

Griffiths, M.D., Wood, R. and Sutherland, I. (1999) *Youth Gambling in the UK.* Proceedings of the National Australian Gambling Society Annual Conference. Adelaide: NAGS.

Griffiths, M.D., Wood, R., Sutherland, T. and Barons, C. (1998) *Adolescent Scratch Card Gambling in the UK.* Invited Paper Presented to The Swedish Gaming Academy, Svenska Spel, Stockholm.

Sutherland, I. (1995) *Can Assessment Tools Designed for Use With Recovering Addicts be Used to Identify Pre-Addicts?* South-West Undergraduate Conference, Bristol University.

Sutherland, I. (1995) *The Development and Application of a Questionnaire to Assess the Changing Personalities of Substance Addicts During the First Year of Recovery.* British Psychological Society (Scottish Branch) Annual General Meeting, Crieff, Scotland.

Sutherland, I. (1996) *Is it Possible to Predict Those at Risk of Addiction?* Psychology Postgraduate Annual General Meeting. Glasgow-Caledonian University.

Sutherland, I. (1996) *The Changing Personalities of Recovering Substance Addicts.* British Psychological Society Annual General Meeting, Brighton.

Sutherland, I. (1997) *Is it Possible to Predict Which Adolescents Are at Risk From Addiction?* Staffordshire Education Authority Symposium on Adolescent Substance Abuse, Stafford.

Sutherland, I. (1997) *The Identification of Adolescents at Risk From Addiction.* Addiction Research Group Conference, University of Wales, Swansea.

Sutherland, I. (1997) *The Identification of Adolescents at Risk From Addiction.* Trust for the Study of Adolescence Summer Symposium. London.

Sutherland, I. (1998) *The Development of an Instrument to Assess The Vulnerability of Individuals to Substance Misuse.* The National Role of Crucial Assessment Conference. Leeds.

Sutherland, I. and Willner, P. (1997) *The Link Between Neuroticism, Social Influences and the Onset of Substance Use in Adolescents.* British Psychological Society Annual General Meeting. Edinburgh.

Sutherland, I. and Willner, P. (1997) *The Role of Alcohol in Adolescent Substance Abuse: No Alcohol, no Drug Misuse?* American Psychological Society Annual General Meeting. Chicago.

Sutherland, I., Willner, P. and Gough, R. (1997) *The Role of Alcohol in Adolescent Substance Abuse: No Alcohol, no Drug Misuse?* British Psvchological Society Annual General Meeting. Edinburgh.

Books/Manuals

Sutherland, I. (1997) The Manual for The Substance Abuse Susceptibility Index, The Psychological Cornoration, London.

Grants

Shepherd, J.P. Sutherland I., et al. (2002) Word, £187,651, A Randomised Controlled Trial of a Brief Alcohol Intervention in a Judicial Setting.

Sutherland, I. (2001) Thomas Bequest Fund, £300 Awarded for Research Into Accident and Emergency Department Recorded Violence Data.

Sutherland, I. (2001) William Morgan Bequest Fund, £300 Awarded for Research Into Accident and Emergency Department Recorded Violence Data and Linking With Oversees Research Institutes.

Willner, P. and Sutherland, I. (1997) AERC £87,000.